Acrobat X

JOHN DEUBERT

 Peachpit Press

Visual QuickStart Guide
Adobe Acrobat X
John Deubert

Peachpit Press
1249 Eighth Street
Berkeley, CA 94710
510/524-2178
510/524-2221 (fax)

Find us on the Web at: www.peachpit.com
To report errors, please send a note to errata@peachpit.com
Peachpit Press is a division of Pearson Education

Editor: Becky Morgan
Production Editor: Danielle Foster
Copyeditor: Anne Marie Walker
Compositor: Myrna Vladic
Indexer: FireCrystal Communications
Cover design: Peachpit Press

ISBN-13 978-0-321-74375-6
ISBN-10   0-321-74375-X

9 8 7 6 5 4 3 2 1

Printed and bound in the United States of America

Dedication

For (in order of height) Barbara, Elizabeth, Gigi, and Julia.

Acknowledgements

In updating an existing book, pretty much everyone else works harder than the author, whose name goes on the cover. Accordingly, I celebrate everyone who slaved over this
project but who *doesn't* get to put her name in a highly visible place.

While this book could arguably have been updated without me, it absolutely wouldn't be in your hands without the following people: Becky Morgan, my Editor, who combines thoughtfulness, vigilance, and a surprising lack of sarcasm when my prose seems to have been poorly translated from the original Klingon; Production Editor Danielle Foster made sure that I actually sent in all the bits and pieces that go into the book; Copyeditor Anne Marie Walker kept my text from straying too horribly far from standard English; Compositor Myrna Vladic assembled the disparate and ill-matching collection of images and chunks of text into a remarkably nice-looking book; and Indexer Emily Glossbrenner did a wonderful job at a task requiring both creativity and a tolerance for tedium.

My heartfelt thanks to everyone!

At home, as always, I thank my wife for her patience when I turn into He Who Doesn't Move for days at a time.

Table of Contents

Introduction

You have to give Adobe credit. There aren't many companies that have managed to change the world once, let alone twice. In 1985, Adobe introduced PostScript, which became the rock on which the entire electronic publishing industry was built; they forever changed the world of professional printing. In 1994, Adobe launched the first version of Acrobat, whose file format, PDF, is now the basis for modern electronic distribution of all manner of documents.

PDF files are used by everyone who creates or receives documents in the modern world. CEOs, secretaries, artists, railway-station managers, hemp-wearing individuals who create crystal-based healing jewelry; everybody with a computer sends and receives documents as PDF, and uses some flavor of Adobe software to read them.

Acrobat X is the newest incarnation of Adobe Systems' software for viewing, managing, and manipulating PDF files. This version of Acrobat reflects years and years (and years!) of Adobe's technological development and end-user experience.

The emphasis in this version of Acrobat is usability. Adobe has rethought much of Acrobat's interface to make it more streamlined and easily explored. Creating forms, sending files out for review, and combining PDF files into a single document is smoother and easier than ever.

In addition, it is easier to discover features of Acrobat X that you never knew existed. Did you know that you can measure distances and areas on scale drawings, or that you can conduct a live video conference to discuss a document? Adobe also provides a free online service, Acrobat.com, to let you share any kind of file—not just PDFs—with other people.

Acrobat X is designed to ensure that if you need a feature, you will find it. "Do what you need to, faster and easier" was clearly a primary design goal for this newest Acrobat. For my taste, this is the easiest-to-use Acrobat to come along for years.

How to use this book

This book describes the purpose and use of Acrobat X's most important features, new and old. Like all Visual QuickStart Guides, this book emphasizes the practical application of the program's features and provides step-by-step instructions on how to use those features. To help work through those steps, you can download a set of pre-built PDF files that you can use as examples as you explore the tools in Acrobat X. These files are available on the book's web page: www.peachpit.com/acrobatxvqs.

Starting With Acrobat

Let's start with the basics: How to open Acrobat, what you'll be looking at when you do so, and how to quit the application. We'll also see how to customize some of the Acrobat user interface.

The goal in this chapter is to get oriented and become comfortable with the layout of the software's windows.

In This Chapter

Launching and Quitting Acrobat X

You open and quit Acrobat X the way you open or close any application on the Macintosh or in Windows.

To open Acrobat X:

- Do one of the following:
  - ▸ Double-click the Acrobat X application icon .
  - ▸ Double-click a PDF file icon.
  - ▸ On the Macintosh, click the Spotlight icon, type *Acro*, and then click on Acrobat X when it appears in the list of hits.
  - ▸ In Windows, choose Acrobat X in the Start menu's All Programs submenu.

In all cases, Acrobat X launches.

If you started Acrobat by double-clicking a PDF file icon, Acrobat presents you with that document's first page.

If you double-clicked the Acrobat X application icon, you will see the Acrobat Welcome screen ⑧. We'll talk more about this window in a moment.

To quit Acrobat X:

- Do one of the following:
  - ▸ On the Macintosh, choose Acrobat > Quit Acrobat.
  - ▸ In Windows, choose File > Exit.
  - ▸ On either platform, press Ctrl-Q (Command-Q).
  - ▸ In Windows, close all open document windows.

You can also unplug the computer or whap it with a mallet—a bit harsh, but effective.

Ⓐ The most common way to start Acrobat X is to double-click the icon of either the application or a PDF file.

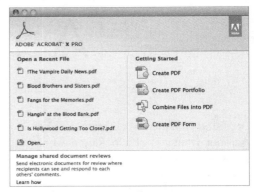

Ⓑ When first opened, Acrobat presents you with the Welcome screen.

Using the Welcome Screen

When you launch Acrobat X without opening a document, Acrobat presents you with its Welcome screen ⓑ.

The Welcome screen provides convenient access to the most commonly used Acrobat activities. The left side of the window offers clickable links to the five most recently opened PDF files.

The rest of the window presents a series of links that execute particular actions. These are reasonably self-descriptive, but for the record here is an explanation of each:

- **Open** (at the bottom of the recent-files list) lets you open a PDF file. You can also open an image or other type of file and Acrobat will do its best to convert it to PDF. We'll talk about this in detail in Chapter 2, "Viewing a Document."

- **Create PDF** lets you create a PDF file from a TIFF, Word, or other file. You can even open a PDF file and convert *that* to PDF, though it's not especially exciting. (See Chapter 4, "Making PDF Files.")

- **Create PDF Portfolio** lets you combine a group of files (PDFs, images, spreadsheets, etc.) into a PDF package called a portfolio. (See Chapter 6, "PDF Portfolios.")

- **Combine Files into PDF** lets you combine a set of files into a single PDF file. This is similar to the Portfolio link except the result is a vanilla PDF file. (See Chapter 4, "Making PDF Files.")

continues on next page

- **Create PDF Form** lets you create a PDF file with interactive form fields. (See Chapter 14, "Creating Forms with Acrobat Pro.")

Some people don't like to be faced with the Welcome screen every time they launch Acrobat. On the Macintosh, you can tell Acrobat not to show the Welcome screen in the Preferences dialog. We discuss the Preferences dialog at the end of this chapter.

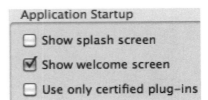

A Mac users (but not Windows users, go figure) can turn off the Welcome screen by deselecting this check box in the General Preferences.

To turn off the Welcome screen (Macintosh only):

1. Choose Acrobat > Preferences.

    Acrobat displays its Preferences dialog. (See the figure at the chapter's end.)

2. Select the General Preferences.

3. Deselect the Show Welcome Screen check box A.

4. Click OK.

Windows users can't do without the Welcome screen because the Windows version of Acrobat must have at least one window open at all times; closing the last window closes the application.

TIP **I prefer the Welcome screen because roughly 83 percent of the time it gives me quick access to exactly what I want to do.**

Examining the Initial Screen

When you open a document in Acrobat, you see a window similar to **Ⓐ**. The layout of this window is significantly different from early versions of Acrobat. In most cases the layout has been simplified and streamlined.

The main parts of a document window are as follows:

- **Drag bar.** This is a standard Macintosh or Windows drag bar. It contains the name of the PDF document and all the controls you'll find in any application's document window, including the Close, Minimize, and Zoom buttons.

continues on next page

Menu bar   Quick Tools toolbar   Favorites toolbar

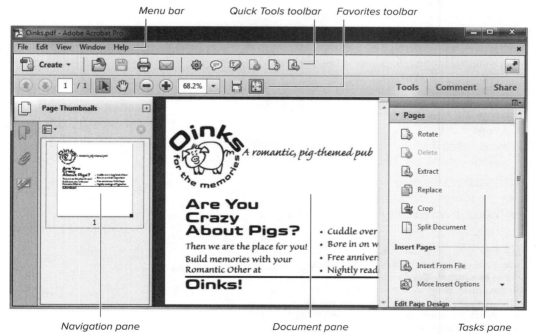

Navigation pane   Document pane   Tasks pane

Ⓐ When you open a document in Acrobat X, you will be looking at the new, efficient, streamlined interface.

- **Document pane.** This is where Acrobat displays the pages of your PDF document.

- **Menu bar.** The location of the menu bar conforms to your platform's standards. In Windows, the menu bar is at the top of the document window; on the Macintosh, the menu bar runs along the top of the screen.

- **Toolbars.** In Acrobat X, each document window has two toolbars. The top toolbar is called the Quick Tools toolbar; the bottom toolbar is the Favorites toolbar.

  Note that the myriad toolbars that existed in earlier versions of Acrobat are gone; now there are only two toolbars and they are always visible.

- **Tasks pane.** This pane replaces the 147½ toolbars in previous versions of Acrobat. The Tasks pane is made up of a series of Tool panels; each contains a set of tools you can use with a PDF file. This is where you find the tools for commenting, redacting, and otherwise working with a PDF file.

- **Navigation pane.** This contains a number of icons that, when clicked, reveal a variety of tools for moving around in the document, including clickable page thumbnails and bookmarks.

The toolbars, Tasks pane, and Navigation pane are all highly customizable, and it's easy to load them up with your favorite tools.

TIP The drag bar's Close button behaves differently on the Macintosh and Windows. On the Macintosh, the Close button closes the document window but doesn't exit the Acrobat application. In Windows, if no other documents are open, the Close button closes the document and also exits Acrobat. These are standard behaviors on the Macintosh and in Windows.

Examining the Menus

Acrobat X has greatly simplified its system of menus from the large collection of menus in earlier versions. There are now only five menus at the top of each document window in Windows; on the Macintosh, six menus span the screen **A**. You'll eventually be using items from each of these menus. For the moment, let's look at each menu and see what kinds of tasks they make possible:

- **Acrobat menu.** This Macintosh-only menu contains items that affect the operation of the application as a whole.

  In particular, this is where you set the application preferences and exit Acrobat on the Macintosh.

- **File menu.** This menu lists the commands to Open, Close, Save, and otherwise manipulate the PDF files on your computer's hard disk. This menu is similar to the File menu in other applications. In Windows, this is where you exit the application.

- **Edit menu.** This is a reasonably standard Macintosh and Windows Edit menu. It contains Cut, Copy, Paste, and other common commands. In Windows, this is where you set the application preferences.

- **View menu.** The commands in this menu let you change how Acrobat presents your documents. You can choose items such as page display and zoom level. This is also where you specify which Navigation panes are visible.

- **Window menu.** This menu lets you specify the details of document windows. For example, you can tile or stack the windows, bring a particular document to the front, and zoom to full screen.

- **Help menu.** This menu provides access to Acrobat's extensive help system, which includes a full Acrobat reference. It also lets you check for updates and register your Acrobat software.

TIP The Help menu is your friend. Adobe has done a remarkably good job of describing the purpose and use of every part of Acrobat. You should definitely take advantage of this information at every opportunity. Not sure what a trusted identity is? Need to add page numbers to a PDF file? The Help system will guide you through the process (though not, I hasten to add, with this volume's style, panache, and sense of excitement).

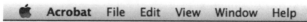

A Acrobat X has half as many menus as its immediate predecessor. This is good.

Examining the Tasks Pane

The Tasks pane is new to Acrobat X and is, without question, my favorite single addition to the program. This pane replaces the array of toolbars that plagued the last several versions of the program.

The Tasks pane resides on the right side of each document window but is initially hidden so as not to take up unnecessary screen real estate. What you initially see is a set of three headings toward the upper right of the window: Tools, Comment, and Share **A**. These are the clickable names of the three panes that collectively make up the Tasks pane; each *subpane* contains tools of a particular type:

- The **Tools pane** contains a wide-ranging set of tools for everything from cropping pages to creating an interactive form.
- The **Comment pane** allows you to attach sticky notes, circles, arrows, paragraphs of text, and other annotations to a page.
- The **Share pane** lets you distribute your PDF file to one or more recipients using email or Acrobat.com.

We'll be talking in detail about the tools in these panes as we go through the book.

When you click on one of these names, Acrobat reveals that pane and its component tools, which are organized into *panels* **B**. Each panel can be opened or closed by clicking on the panel's name.

There are several Tasks pane panels, most of which you may never use. Fortunately, you can remove all the panels that don't apply to you.

A At the upper right of each document window are the triggers for the Tasks pane's three component subpanes.

B Tools in the Tasks pane are organized into a series of panels that can be opened or closed according to what you're doing at the moment.

C Clicking the tiny menu button at the top of the Tasks pane lets you choose which panels you want to display.

To specify which panels should appear in a Tasks pane:

1. Make a Tasks pane visible, if necessary, by clicking on its name in the document window.

2. Click the small menu icon at the right side of the bar at the top of the pane **C**.

   Acrobat displays a pop-up menu of all the panels available for that pane. Visible panels will have a check mark next to their names.

3. Select a panel whose visibility you want to change.

   Acrobat reverses the visibility of that panel and closes the pop-up menu.

4. Repeat steps 2 and 3 for each panel you want to modify.

You'll know all the Tasks panes in depth by the end of this book. Let's start the process by looking at the panels—the sets of tools— that reside in each of the three panes.

TIP By default, only one Tool panel can be open at a time; open one panel and the previous one closes. You can change this behavior by selecting Allow Multiple Panels in the Tasks pane's pop-up menu **C**. Now you can have as many panels open as your heart desires. (I prefer the one-panel-at-a-time mode.)

TIP The Share pane has only one panel, so of course it doesn't offer you a choice of which panels should be available.

Examining the Tools pane

The Tools pane is an eclectic collection of tools that give you access to nearly every Acrobat feature except commenting on and sharing a document 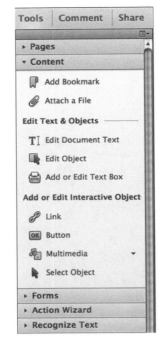. The panels that live in this pane include:

- **Pages.** Rotate, delete, insert, and otherwise manipulate the pages in the PDF file.

- **Content.** Create bookmarks, add clickable links, and touch up text or objects.

- **Forms.** Add or modify interactive form fields.

- **Protection.** Encrypt, redact, or sanitize (really) a document.

- **Sign & Certify.** Add an electronic signature or certify the validity of a document.

- **Recognize Text.** Use optical character recognition to convert a scanned document to searchable text.

- **Action Wizard.** Add an automated action.

- **Document Processing.** Add page numbers, optimize images, and automatically create or remove links.

- **Print Production.** Preflight, add printer marks, and preview overprinting.

- **JavaScript.** Edit and debug the JavaScripts attached to the document.

- **Accessibility.** Check a document for accessibility and add information allowing accessible reading software to use the document.

- **Analyze.** Measure scaled areas and distances within your PDF file.

D The Tools pane holds tools that apply to a variety of tasks, from rearranging pages to applying password protection.

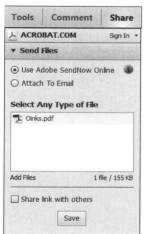

E The Comment pane lets you add annotations to a page. At this point, Acrobat supports a huge array of annotation types.

F The Share pane lets you easily email your document to a list of people or share it online using Acrobat.com.

TIP Acrobat.com is a big deal. Really. This free(!) service lets you share any file or collection of files with a group of recipients of your choice. Acrobat makes it convenient to share PDF files, but you can actually upload any kind of file to Acrobat.com free of charge. Authorized personnel can then download files to their computers. Have I mentioned that it's free?

Examining the Comment pane

The Comment pane contains the tools you will use to annotate a PDF file **E**. Acrobat's collection of annotation tools has experienced years of evolution, and this latest incarnation is powerful and easy to use. We discuss these in detail in Chapters 7–9. (It's a big subject!)

The panels available in this pane include:

- **Annotations.** Place notes, mark up text, and apply a virtual rubber stamp.

- **Drawing Markups.** Draw circles, squares, arrows, and other graphic objects to call attention to particular places on the page.

- **Review.** Conduct a review of a document, sending it around to a list of participants for comment and approval.

- **Comments List.** Examine and search through a list of all the comments in the document.

Examining the Share pane

The tools in the Share Pane let you, well, share a PDF file with one or more people **F**. You can automatically attach a document to an email or share the file using Acrobat.com.

At the top of this pane is a link inviting you to sign in to Acrobat.com. (Acrobat.com is a free service provided by Adobe; see Chapter 5 for a *lot* more detail.)

The Share pane has only one panel:

- **Send Files.** This panel has all the tools you need to share your document. Acrobat will either attach the file to an email or upload it to Acrobat.com.

Using the Toolbars

Acrobat X's toolbars grew to an alarming extent over the years. Each version of Acrobat added a new collection of toolbars to accommodate new features. Acrobat 9 had 14 toolbars! The Acrobat design team evidently decided that enough was considerably too much.

Acrobat X has only *two* always-present toolbars stacked one above the other at the top of each document window: Ⓐ

- The upper **Quick Tools** toolbar contains a selection of commands from the Tasks pane.

- The lower **Favorites** toolbar holds zoom, navigation, and other tools that have no equivalent in the Tasks pane.

These toolbars are initially populated with a spare set of tools that allow essential file activities, simple annotation, and basic navigation. For everything else, you need to go to the Tasks pane—at least, initially.

Here's the secret to making Acrobat X maximally useful: customization. Acrobat X's toolbars are nearly blank slates; you can place in them any tools from the Tasks pane that you want, according to which tools you use the most.

Nearly everything you can do in Acrobat can be added as a tool to one or the other of the toolbars. You should move to the Quick Tools toolbar all the Tasks pane tools you use frequently. You should load up the Favorites toolbar with your favorite zoom and navigation tools.

After a while, most of your routine activities will be immediately at hand in the toolbars.

Ⓐ Acrobat's toolbars cannot be removed or rearranged. Don't spend time trying.

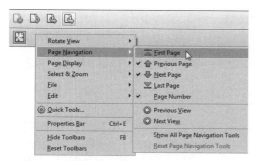

Ⓐ Right-click (Control-click) either toolbar to change the tools available in Favorites.

Customizing the Toolbars

Adobe intended that everyone's toolbars would be unique, reflecting personal needs and preferences. Add to the toolbars the tools you use often; remove those tools you use only once in a blue moon. When your toolbars are properly loaded, you should rarely have to go to the Tasks pane.

TIP Each tool that you add goes to a specific toolbar, depending on the nature of that tool. Tools that appear in the Tasks pane go to the Quick Tools toolbar; everything else goes to the Favorites toolbar. You cannot change this behavior.

To change the tools in the Favorites toolbar:

1. Right-click (Control-click) the Favorites toolbar.

   You will see a hierarchical pop-up menu listing all the tools you can add to the Favorites toolbar **Ⓐ**. Tools that already reside in the toolbar are displayed with a check mark.

2. Select a tool to add or remove.

TIP In step 1, you can also right-click (Control-click) the Quick Tools toolbar, but you have to avoid clicking its tool buttons or you'll get the "remove from Quick Tools" menu.

TIP Acrobat's default collection of Page Navigation tools is unaccountably sparse; you really want to add all the Page Navigation tools (visible in **Ⓐ**) to the toolbar. You can do this quickly by selecting Show All Page Navigation Tools in the hierarchical pop-up menu.

To add a tool to or remove a tool from the Quick Tools toolbar:

1. To add a tool to the Quick Tools toolbar right-click (Control-click) the tool and select Add to Quick Tools from the context menu **B**.

2. To remove a button from the toolbar, right-click (Control-click) the tool and select Remove from Quick Tools **B**.

Rearranging the Quick Tools toolbar

You can do more with the Quick Tools toolbar than just add or remove tools. You can rearrange the tools and add dividers. You do this—as well as add and remove tools—in the Customize Quick Tools dialog.

To customize the Quick Tools toolbar:

1. Right-click (Control-click) anywhere in the two toolbars except on a Quick Tools tool.

   A context menu appears **C**.

2. Select Quick Tools.

   Acrobat displays the Customize Quick Tools dialog **D**.

   On the left is a hierarchical list of all the Tasks pane tools, categorized by panel. On the right is a list of tools that currently reside in the toolbar.

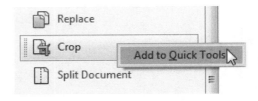

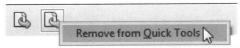

B Add a tool to the Quick Tools toolbar by clicking the tool in the Tasks pane (top). Remove a tool from the toolbar by right-clicking (Control-clicking) it (bottom).

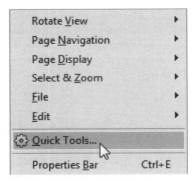

C You open the Customize Quick Tools dialog box from the context menu you get by right-clicking (Control-clicking) the toolbar.

3. Add a tool to the Quick Tools toolbar by selecting the tool in the list on the left and clicking the right arrow button.

4. Remove a tool by selecting the tool in the list on the right and clicking the left arrow button.

5. Change the position of a tool by selecting the tool in the list on the right and dragging it to the position you prefer.

6. Add a divider to the toolbar by clicking the middle button and then clicking in the list on the right.

7. When you're satisfied with the Quick Tools toolbar arrangement, click OK.

TIP If you select one of the panel names in the list on the left (such as **Pages** or **Content** in ⓓ), Acrobat will add all the tools in that panel to the toolbar.

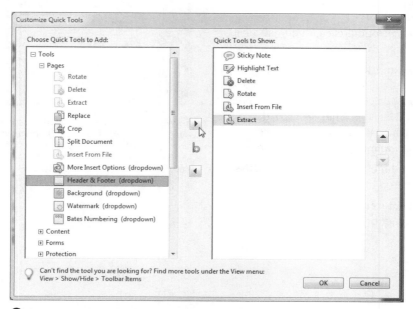

ⓓ The Customize Quick Tools dialog lets you change and rearrange the collection of tools in the Quick Tools toolbar.

Working with Navigation Panes

Acrobat's navigation panes, along the left edge of every document window, provide you with a variety of ways to move around in your document.

These panes are initially retracted, showing only a column of icons—one for each available pane **A**. When opened, a pane allows you to move around within your document in a specific way, such as moving from page to page using thumbnails, moving among the document's bookmarks, and so on **B**.

Most of the navigation panes have a specialized purpose and won't be covered in this book. Acrobat's default available panes are probably the most useful:

- The **Page Thumbnails** pane presents thumbnail views of each page in the document. Double-clicking a thumbnail takes you to that page.

- The **Bookmarks** pane lists all the bookmarks placed in the document. Bookmarks form a clickable table of contents for the PDF file. In Chapter 12, "Adding Simple Navigation Features," you'll learn how to make and use bookmarks.

- The **Attachments** pane lists all files that are attached to the document.

- The **Signatures** pane lists all the document's electronic signatures.

A The navigation panes are initially closed and are evident only as a set of icons at the left of the document window.

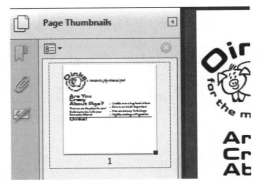

B When you click a navigation pane icon, the pane opens. Here, the Page Thumbnails pane displays a clickable thumbnail of each page.

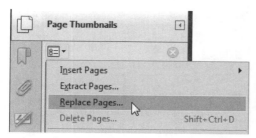

C Clicking the little menu icon at the top of a navigation pane yields a menu of commands specific to that pane.

D By choosing View > Show/Hide > Navigation Panes, you can specify which navigation panes you want visible.

To open and close a navigation pane:

1. Click the tab of a closed navigation pane to open it.

   Acrobat opens the navigation pane.

2. Click the tab of an open pane to close it again.

   The navigation pane collapses down to a tab.

TIP The pane panel has a tiny menu icon that, when clicked, displays a pop-up menu of commands appropriate to the current pane **C**. The collection of commands in this menu varies from one navigation pane to another.

Acrobat defines a large number of navigation panes, most of which aren't initially visible. It's easy to choose which panes you want to display.

To customize the list of navigation panes:

- Choose the pane you want to make visible by choosing View > Show/Hide > Navigation Panes and selecting a pane from the submenu **D**.

   Acrobat toggles the visibility of the navigation tab you choose; if it's visible, it will become hidden, and vice versa.

TIP If you want to get back to basics, you can choose View > Show/Hide > **Navigation Panes** > **Reset Panes** and Acrobat will set the navigation panes back to the default collection.

Setting Preferences

Like all applications, Acrobat maintains a set of preferences that determine how the application should behave when you start a session. This can include such items as the default zoom, the color to be used for comments, and whether Acrobat should report distances in pixels, inches, or centimeters.

Some of the tasks in this book require you to set relevant preferences.

To set Acrobat's preferences:

1. On the Macintosh, choose Acrobat > Preferences. In Windows, choose Edit > Preferences.

   Acrobat displays the Preferences dialog **A**.

2. Click a category name from the list on the left side of the dialog **B**.

   Acrobat presents the controls that apply to that category.

3. Make whatever changes you want to the Preference controls in that category.

4. Repeat steps 2 and 3 for as many categories as you want.

5. Click OK.

> **TIP** In your idle moments, you should browse the controls available in the Preferences dialog. It may not sound entertaining, but you'll be surprised by how much you can learn about an application's capabilities from its preferences.

A Acrobat has an amazing number of Preference controls. You may want to spend some time rummaging around among them; it's amazing what you can learn from preferences.

B Acrobat's Preference controls are split into 34 categories. Click a category name in the list to see the corresponding controls.

2

Viewing a Document

Once you've launched Acrobat and have become familiar with its interface, you're ready to navigate the pages of an open document. This chapter describes the tools in Acrobat X that you use to view a PDF document. We'll look at some routine functions, such as all the ways to move from page to page and how to zoom in and out, as well as some of Acrobat's more exotic capabilities, such as measuring the length and area of items on the page.

In This Chapter

Opening a PDF File

The most basic activity you can carry out in Acrobat is opening a PDF file. You can do this several ways; most of them are identical to the way you open files in other applications.

To open a file from the Finder or Windows Explorer:

Do either of the following:

- Double-click the icon of a PDF file.
- Drag the icon of a PDF file to the Acrobat application icon.

To open a file from the Welcome screen:

1. Click the Open link at the bottom of the list of recent files **Ⓐ**.

   Acrobat presents you with the standard select-a-file dialog.

2. Navigate to the file you want to open, and click OK.

Of course, if the file you want happens to appear in the Welcome screen's list of recent files, you can simply click the file's name and Acrobat will open it.

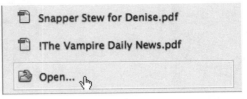

Ⓐ One way of opening a file on your hard disk is to click the Open link in the Welcome screen.

B You can also open a file on your hard disk by clicking the Open File tool in the toolbar.

To open a file from the File menu:

1. Choose File > Open (Ctrl-O/Command-O).

   Acrobat presents you with the standard select-a-file dialog.

2. Navigate to the file you want to open, and click OK.

To open a file from the Quick Tools toolbar:

1. Click the Open File icon in the Quick Tools toolbar **B**.

   Acrobat presents you with the standard select-a-file dialog.

2. Navigate to the file you want to open, and click OK.

TIP You can also open a recently used file by selecting it in the File > Recent Files submenu or clicking it in the Welcome screen.

Moving from Page to Page

After you've opened your document, you'll want to move around among the pages. You have several ways to do so; most of them are familiar from other applications.

To move to the next or previous page:

Do one of the following:

- Press the right or left arrow key on your keyboard to move to the next page or previous page, respectively.

- Click the Previous Page or Next Page button (the up or down arrow) in the Favorites toolbar **A**.

- Press the Page Down or Page Up key on your keyboard.

To move to a particular page:

Do either of the following:

- Type your target page number into the Page Number field in the toolbar **A**.

- Click the Pages navigation tab to expose the Pages navigation pane, and then double-click the thumbnail of your desired page **B**.

To move to the first or last page:

- To go to the document's first page, choose View > Page Navigation > First Page **C** or press the Home key.

- To go to the document's last page, choose View > Page Navigation > Last Page or press the End key.

> **TIP** You can add tools to the Favorites toolbar for First Page and Last Page. I recommend you do so; they are very handy. Chapter 1 tells you how to add tools to a toolbar.

A The Favorites toolbar has arrow buttons for moving to the next and previous page, and a text field into which you can type a page number.

B You can also go to a page by clicking its thumbnail in the Page Thumbnails pane.

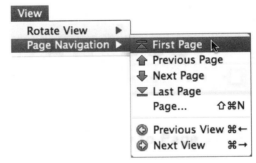

C You can move to the first or last page in the document by selecting the appropriate item in the Page Navigation submenu. You can also add tools for these actions to the Favorites toolbar.

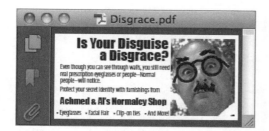

A A view in Acrobat is a combination of a document, page, location on the page, and zoom level. Thus, zooming in on a page takes you to a new view.

B You should add the Next and Previous View tools to the Favorites toolbar; you'll use them all the time!

Moving from View to View

A *view* in Acrobat parlance is a combination of a document, a page within that document, a location on that page, and a zoom level. You change to a new view whenever you go to a new page, zoom in or out, or open a new document **A**.

Acrobat has menu items and associated key shortcuts for moving to the previous and next views. If you jump ahead 15 pages by double-clicking a thumbnail, the Previous View command returns you to your original page.

These controls are very handy.

To move to the previous or next view:

Do either of the following:

- Choose View > Page Navigation > Previous View, or View > Page Navigation > Next View.

- Press Ctrl-left (Command-left) arrow key or Ctrl-right (Command-right) arrow key on your keyboard.

TIP I recommend that you add to the Favorites toolbar the tools for First and Last Page and for Next and Previous View **B**. These functions are so frequently used that you'll want to make access to them as convenient as possible. Chapter 1 tells you how to add tools to a toolbar.

Zooming In and Out

Acrobat provides a View > Zoom submenu of tools that lets you get a closer look at an area of the page or look at a broader region of the page 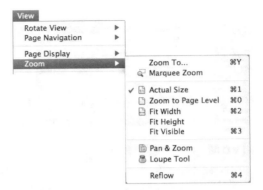. It also has a Select tool in the Favorites toolbar **B**, which you use to edit, examine, and otherwise manipulate items on the page; we will refer to this tool periodically throughout this book.

In Acrobat's default configuration, the Favorites toolbar contains the zoom tools you will use most often **C**. The View > Zoom submenu offers the less frequently used zoom functions. As always, you can add any or all of the zoom tools to the Favorites toolbar.

Acrobat lets you zoom three different ways:

- Zoom by a specific amount.

- Zoom so that the page fits in the document window in a particular way (for example, the page width fills the window).

- Dynamically select the degree of zoom visually.

> **TIP** As I mentioned, you can add the extra zoom tools to the Zoom toolbar. I keep three additional zoom tools in my Favorites toolbar: Marquee Zoom, Actual Size, and Fit Width **D**. See Chapter 1 for a reminder of how to add tools to a toolbar.

A The Zoom menu provides a variety of ways to zoom in to and out of your document. All of these can be added to the Favorites toolbar.

B The Select tool lets you choose text and objects on a PDF page that you want to modify.

C The Favorites toolbar starts out with the most frequently used zoom tools. You can add others.

D I keep three additional zoom tools in my toolbar: Marquee Zoom, Actual Size, and Fit Width. I can't live without them.

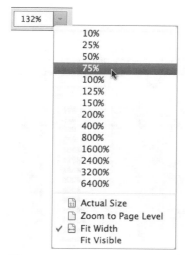

E You can select a zoom amount from the Zoom Amount drop-down menu in the Favorites toolbar.

F You can zoom until the entire page fits in the Acrobat window or until the document page exactly fits across the window's width.

TIP All of the zoom commands are also available in the View > Zoom submenu.

To zoom by a fixed amount:

Do one of the following:

- Click the Zoom In (+) or Zoom Out (–) tool on the Favorites toolbar. Acrobat zooms in to a predetermined zoom level. Starting at 100%, for example, repeated clicks of the + button take you to zooms of 125%, 150%, 200%, and so on up to 6400%.

- Type a zoom percentage in the Favorites toolbar's text field.

- Click the small down arrow next to the Favorites toolbar's text field, and choose a predefined zoom percentage from the resulting Zoom Amount menu **E**.

To zoom the page to fit the document window:

Do one of the following:

- To zoom out until one page fits entirely inside the window **F**, choose Zoom to Page Level from the Zoom Amount menu on the Favorites toolbar **E** or press Ctrl-0 (Command-0).

- To zoom in until the document's pages exactly fit across the width of the window, choose Fit Width from the Zoom Amount menu **E** or press Ctrl-2 (Command-2).

- To zoom until the document's pages exactly fit the height of the window, choose Fit Height from the Zoom Amount menu.

- To zoom until the text and images on your pages exactly fit the document window, choose Fit Visible from the Zoom Amount menu or press Ctrl-3 (Command-3).

- To zoom to 100%, choose Actual Size in the Zoom Amount menu or press Ctrl-1 (Command-1).

The Marquee Zoom tool

The Marquee Zoom tool is the best tool to use when you want to get a better look at a particular part of the page. It lets you intuitively zoom in on a specific area of the page.

To zoom with the Marquee Zoom tool:

1. Choose View > Zoom > Marquee Zoom.

   The mouse pointer turns into a magnifying glass with a plus sign in it .

2. Click in the document window, and drag a rectangle around the area you want to zoom in on **H**.

   Acrobat zooms in until the area you enclosed in the marquee fills the document window **I**.

> **TIP** If you click in the document window without dragging a rectangle, Acrobat zooms in by a predefined amount. The zoomed page will be centered on the point on which you clicked.

> **TIP** You can use the Marquee Zoom tool to zoom out of the page, as well. Repeat the steps in the previous task while holding down the Shift key. Acrobat zooms out, showing you more of the page.

> **TIP** You can get temporary access to the Marquee Zoom tool anytime by holding down Ctrl-spacebar (Command-spacebar) on your keyboard. Acrobat activates the Marquee Zoom feature, allowing you to zoom in on the page. If you also hold down the Alt (Option) key (Ctrl-Alt-spacebar/Command-Option-spacebar), the mouse pointer will temporarily let you zoom out.

> **TIP** I recommend you add the Marquee Zoom tool to your Favorites toolbar; it's one of the most useful zoom tools.

G When you select the Marquee Zoom tool, the mouse pointer turns into a magnifying glass. If you hold the Option key, the magnifying glass acquires a minus sign, indicating it will zoom out.

H To use the Marquee Zoom tool, drag a rectangle around the area you want to examine more closely.

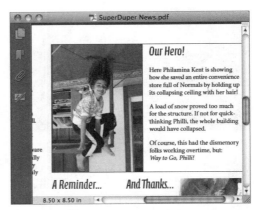

I Acrobat will zoom in until the area you selected with the Marquee Zoom tool fills the window.

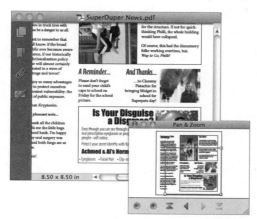

J The Loupe tool lets you drag a target rectangle around the page and view a close-up of the rectangle's contents in a dialog.

K When you click the Pan & Zoom tool, Acrobat presents you with a floating thumbnail view of your page with a target rectangle.

The Loupe tool

The Loupe tool gives you a separate window that displays a close-up of an area in the main document window. This is a very useful tool for checking out the details of several places on the page in quick succession.

To zoom with the Loupe tool:

1. Choose View > Zoom > Loupe Tool.

   The mouse pointer changes to a small crosshair.

2. Click in the document window.

   Acrobat displays a target rectangle in the document window, and a floating Loupe tool window that shows a close-up of whatever is in the rectangle **J**. You can drag this rectangle around the document window to see different parts of the page.

> **TIP** Note that the Loupe tool (and all the other zoom tools) remains activated until you select a different tool in a menu or toolbar. This can be surprising at first.

> **TIP** The Loupe tool floating window has controls that let you specify such things as the degree of magnification and the color of the target rectangle. You can also enlarge the rectangle by dragging its corners.

The Pan & Zoom tool

Another of Acrobat's zoom tools is the Pan & Zoom. This is the opposite of the Loupe tool. Acrobat presents you with a floating window containing a thumbnail view of your page. You drag and resize a target rectangle in the thumbnail, and Acrobat zooms the main document page so that the target rectangle fills the page **K**.

To zoom with the Pan & Zoom tool:

1. Choose View > Zoom > Pan & Zoom Window.

   Acrobat displays a floating Pan & Zoom window containing a thumbnail image of your document page. The floating window also has a target rectangle that corresponds to the area visible in the main window.

2. Resize and move the target rectangle so that it encloses the area on the thumbnail that you want to see up close.

   As you do so, Acrobat continuously updates the document window so that it's filled with the area enclosed by the target rectangle 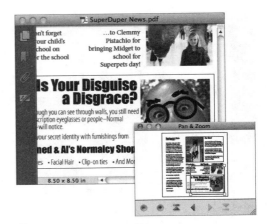.

   You resize the target rectangle by dragging the handles at its corners and sides.

   TIP You can also use the controls on the Pan & Zoom thumbnail window to specify a percentage scale, change the color of the target rectangle, or move from page to page within the document.

L As you move and resize the target rectangle, Acrobat zooms the main document window so the rectangle's contents fill the window.

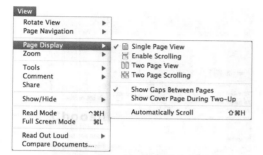

A The Page Display submenu provides a number of ways to arrange your windows on the screen.

B The Favorites toolbar has tools for the commonly used page layout options. As always, you can add more.

C Two of the layouts in the Page Display submenu are Single Page (left) and the awkwardly named Enable Scrolling (right).

Choosing a Page Display

Acrobat can organize your document's pages within the document window a number of ways, such as one page at a time or side by side. These display layouts are in the View > Page Display submenu **A**; some of them are available by default in the Favorites toolbar as well **B**.

To change the page layout:

Do either of the following:

- Select the desired layout by choosing View > Page Display.

- Click a layout button in the Favorites toolbar.

By default, only two layouts—Single Page and Scrolling—are available in this toolbar. You can add the other layouts to the toolbar; see Chapter 1 for instructions on how to customize a toolbar.

Acrobat page display layouts

The View > Page Display submenu allows you access to the following layouts:

- **Single Page View** displays one page at a time in the document window **C**.

- **Enable Scrolling** displays the pages in the document as a single, scrollable column **C**.

continues on next page

- **Two Page View** displays two pages at a time, side by side 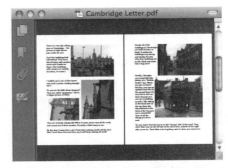.
- **Two Page Scrolling** displays two columns of side-by-side pages **D**.

TIP The Two Page View and Two Page Scrolling layouts are particularly useful for PDF files that are intended to be bound as a book; they allow you to see how the pages will look when the book is open.

TIP If you select Show Cover Page During Two-Up in the View > Page Display submenu, Acrobat displays two-up pages with a blank cover page. The net result of this is to make the first page of the PDF document a right-hand page **E**. This page display can be incredibly useful if your document will be bound, because it shows the actual pairing of the document's pages.

TIP This is cool: If you choose View > Page Display > Automatically Scroll (Ctrl-H/ Command-H), Acrobat will automatically scroll slowly through the document. Just lean back and read the text as it passes before your eyes!

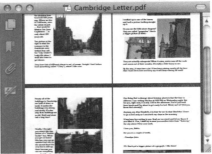

D Two Page View (top) and Two Page Scrolling (bottom) show the pairing of the document's pages. These are useful for seeing how printed documents will look when the pages are bound.

E The Show Cover Page During Two-Up option forces the first page to be a right-hand page, matching the way the document pages will look when bound.

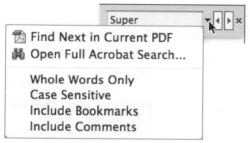

A A small Search Text field appears below the toolbars when you are searching for text. The controls here are a text field (for your search text), a drop-down menu, Previous and Next Find buttons, and an X to end the search.

B Clicking the little down arrow yields a menu of search options.

Searching for Text

Acrobat has an effective mechanism for searching for a particular piece of text within a document. It's similar to the search features in other applications.

You have two distinct mechanisms available to you for finding text in an Acrobat document:

- **Find** looks for text within the current document. Acrobat lets you step through successive instances of the found text one at a time.

- **Advanced Search** looks for text in one or more PDF files in locations you specify on your computer's disk. Acrobat presents you with a clickable list of all the instances of that text within the documents.

To find text in a document:

1. Choose Edit > Find (Ctrl-F/Command-F).

   A small Find box appears, hanging down from the right side of the toolbars **A**.

2. Type into the text field the word or phrase you want to find.

3. Click the little down arrow next to the text field and select the search options you want to use **B**:

   ▸ **Whole Words Only.** Acrobat ignores the text if it's preceded or followed by other alphanumeric characters. Thus, when searching for "wait," Acrobat ignores "waiting."

   ▸ **Case Sensitive.** Acrobat considers case in its search; thus, "axolotl" and "Axolotl" are considered different.

continues on next page

- ▸ **Include Bookmarks**. Acrobat searches the titles of the document's bookmarks as well as page contents. We discuss using bookmarks later in the chapter.

- ▸ **Include Comments**. Acrobat searches comments.

Note that you can also go to the next found instance or open the multiple-file search from this menu.

4. Press the Enter (Return) key. Acrobat searches the document for the text, stops when it finds an instance, and highlights the text on the page **C**.

5. To go to the next instance of the text in the document, click the right arrow button in the Find box **A**.

6. To go to the previous instance of the text, click the left arrow button **A**.

7. To close the Find box, click the X.

TIP The Find feature ignores diacritical marks in its search; for example, Jose, José, and jose are considered identical.

TIP You can add a Find tool to the Favorites toolbar. Just right-click (Control-click) the toolbar and choose Edit > Find **D**.

C When the Find function discovers an instance of the word, it moves the document window so the word is visible and highlights the text on the page.

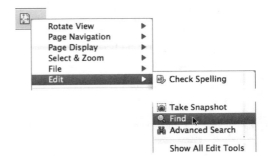

D You can add a Find tool to the Favorites toolbar. Just right-click (Control-click) the toolbar and select Find.

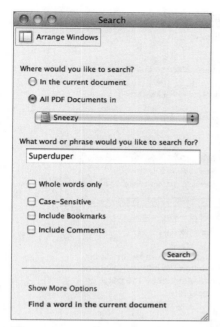

E The Search dialog lets you search for a word or phrase in all the PDF files in a particular location.

F The pop-up menu in the Search dialog lets you specify where Acrobat should look for PDF files in its search.

To search for text in one or more documents:

1. Choose Edit > Advanced Search.

   The Search dialog opens **E**.

2. Type into the text field the word or phrase you want to search.

3. Click one of the radio buttons to specify where Acrobat should search for the text—in the current PDF document or in all PDF documents in a particular location.

   In the latter case, you can choose a location from the pop-up menu **F**.

4. Select the check boxes associated with the options you want for the search **E**.

   continues on next page

5. Click the Search button.

Acrobat searches all the documents for the specified text. It then creates a list showing all the instances it finds 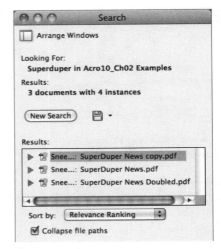.

6. To examine any of the found instances, click that instance in the list.

The document window shows you the found text; if that text resides in a different PDF file, Acrobat opens that file.

7. Click the New Search button to start a new search, or click the dialog's Close button to close the Search dialog.

TIP Note that Acrobat can search all the PDF files on all your disks **F**. This can take a while—a very long while. Go out for coffee; play with the dog; paint the house.

TIP You can save your search results to a PDF or CSV file (the latter is a comma-delimited format used by spreadsheets and database software). Just click the disk icon in the Results dialog **G** and select PDF or CSV from the resulting drop-down menu **H**.

TIP You can add an Advanced Search tool to the Favorites toolbar. Just right-click (Control-click) the toolbar and select Advanced Search **I**.

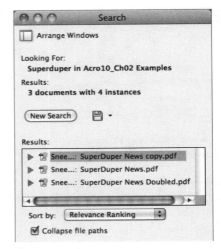

G The Search feature returns a list of all the instances it finds. Click one of the instances to see the page on which it resides.

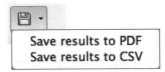

H Clicking the disk button in the Search dialog lets you save your search results to a file.

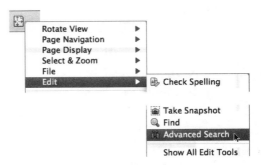

I You can add an Advanced Search tool to the Favorites toolbar. Just right-click (Control-click) the toolbar and select Advanced Search.

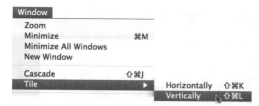

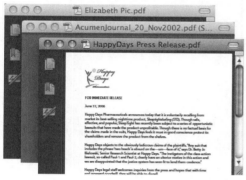

Arranging Documents on the Screen

Acrobat lets you tile or cascade the currently open document windows.

These options are available in the Window menu **A**.

A The Window menu lets you tile or cascade open document windows.

B Cascading the document windows is useful when you want to see only one of them at a time.

C Tiling the windows is helpful when you want all the documents to be visible simultaneously.

To arrange documents on the screen:

Do one of the following:

- Choose Window > Cascade. Acrobat resizes the document windows and offsets them so that the title bars of all the windows are visible **B**.

- Choose Window > Tile > Vertically. Acrobat tiles the windows top to bottom, filling the entire screen **C**.

- Choose Window > Tile > Horizontally. Acrobat tiles the windows across the width of the screen.

Using Read Mode

In Read mode, Acrobat tries to make a document as easy as possible to read onscreen. To do this, Acrobat hides the toolbars and navigation tabs, and zooms the document so that it fits across the width of the document window .

Additionally, when you move the mouse to the bottom of the window, Acrobat presents a heads-up display (HUD) with a variety of useful controls **B**.

A In Read mode, Acrobat hides all toolbars and panes, and zooms the document so that its width stretches across the window.

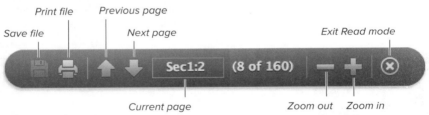

B Read mode's heads-up display allows you to navigate the pages.

C Enter Read mode by clicking the double-arrow button at the right end of the toolbars.

To enter and exit Read mode:

1. To enter Read mode, choose View > Read Mode or click the double-arrow button at the right end of the Quick Tools toolbar **C**.

2. To exit Read mode, choose View > Read Mode, press the Escape key, or click the "X" in the heads-up display **B**.

To navigate pages in Read mode:

1. To move forward one page in the document, do either of the following:

   ▸ Press the right arrow key on your keyboard.

   ▸ Click the down arrow in the heads-up display.

2. To move back one page in the document, do either of the following:

   ▸ Press the left arrow key on your keyboard.

   ▸ Click the up arrow in the heads-up display.

3. To move forward or backward one screen in the document, do either of the following:

   ▸ Press the Page Up or Page Down keys.

   ▸ Spin your scroll wheel.

4. To go to the first or last page in your document, press the Home or End keys.

5. To go to a specific page in the document, type the page number into the text field in the heads-up display.

TIP Read mode is particularly useful for reading documents that were originally formatted for print. It makes it easier to read the small text used in such documents.

TIP If you are working on a Macintosh laptop, you may not be aware that you do, indeed, have Home, End, Page Up, and Page Down keys. Hold down the "fn" key and press the left, right, up, or down arrow to get these keys. You're welcome.

Using Links and Bookmarks

Acrobat gives the author of a PDF file the ability to add navigation features that make it easy for a reader to move around a document. In Chapter 12, you'll learn how to create these navigation features. Here, you'll learn to use them when viewing a PDF document.

Note that the author must build these features into the PDF document for them to be available to the reader.

Using links

Links in Acrobat work just like links in Web pages. You click them, and the document does something: moves you to another location in the document, plays a movie, or performs some other activity determined by the document designer.

It's up to the creator of the PDF file to make a page's links visible to the reader. You will generally see the same range of visual clues that you find on a Web page, such as blue text and button icons .

TIP As in a Web browser, you can always tell when the mouse cursor is hovering over a link because the cursor changes to a pointing finger.

TIP The destination associated with a link may be in a different file. Some documents are distributed as a set of PDF files, one for each chapter; clicking a link in a Table of Contents file takes you to the file that contains that topic.

TIP A link's destination can also be a Web site. When you click such a link, Acrobat opens that Web page in your browser.

Milwaukee Cheese Cutters Association
(Click here for info.)

A Links and buttons in PDF pages usually look like those in their Web page equivalents.

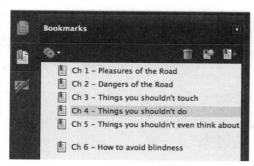

B Clicking the Bookmarks tab exposes the document's bookmarks.

Using bookmarks

Bookmarks reside in the Bookmarks navigation pane, one of the tabs along the left side of your document windows. The bookmarks form a clickable table of contents provided by the document's author.

Clicking a bookmark takes you to a predetermined location in the document.

To use a document's bookmarks:

1. Click the Bookmarks tab to open the Bookmarks navigation pane, if necessary.

   You see all of the document's bookmarks **B**.

2. Click a bookmark.

   Acrobat takes you to the location associated with that bookmark.

Measuring Sizes and Areas

Acrobat provides a set of tools that you can use to measure the sizes and areas of items on a page. These measurements can be reported in any units you desire. You specify a scale (so many millimeters equals so many feet, for example), and Acrobat reports its results in real units. This makes these tools extremely useful for working with maps, floor plans, and other scale drawings.

You access the measuring tools from the Analyze panel in the Tasks pane **A**. Open the Analyze panel by clicking its name, and then click Measuring Tool. Acrobat displays the Measurement palette **B**.

The Measurement palette

The Measurement palette has three measurement tools and four buttons for "snap types." We'll discuss the tools first and then talk about what a snap type is.

The three measurement tools on the right side of the palette **B** are as follows (from left to right in the palette):

- The **Distance tool** is used for measuring the distance between two points.

- The **Perimeter tool** is used for measuring the length of an area's border on the page.

- The **Area tool** is used for measuring the area of a region on the page.

A The measuring tools live in the Analyze panel in the Tasks pane.

B The Measurement palette contains three measurement tools on the right and four Snap Types buttons.

The Snap Types buttons on the left side of the Measurement palette specify that when you click on the page with a measuring tool, the cursor should move, or snap, to the nearest significant point. The buttons let you specify any combination of four types of "significant points," all reasonably self-explanatory (from left to right in the palette):

- Snap to **Paths**
- Snap to **Endpoints**
- Snap to **Midpoint**
- Snap to **Intersection**

TIP All the snap types are turned on by default. I can think of no reason why they shouldn't be left on. Generally, you are measuring something that is drawn on the page, and the Snap Types feature is extremely convenient.

TIP A measuring tool will snap to a path, endpoint, and so on only if the tool is already within a few screen pixels of that point when you click. This is a good thing, because having a tool jump to an endpoint that is halfway across the page gets really annoying after the thirtieth time.

To measure the distance between two points:

1. Select the Distance tool in the Measurement palette.

   The mouse pointer becomes a crosshair, and the Measuring Info floating window opens **C**.

2. Click once on the starting point for the distance you want to measure.

   Now, wherever you move your mouse, Acrobat draws a double-arrow line that shows the distance between the mouse's current position and the starting point **D**. The Measuring Info window also continually reports the distance from the starting point to the mouse's current position.

3. Click the second endpoint for the distance you want to measure.

   The endpoints of the distance you want to measure are now frozen in place. The crosshair is still "live," and now lets you position the double arrow against the page background.

4. Move the crosshair around until the double arrow is positioned where you want it, and click a final time to end the measurement.

   The Measuring Info window reports the distance between your endpoints **C**. The double arrows remain on the page as a special annotation called a *measurement markup* **E**.

Distance Tool
Distance: 0.23 in
  Angle: 43.63
ΔX: 0.16 in   ΔY: 0.16 in
Scale Ratio: 1 in = 1 in

C The Measuring Info window provides ongoing measurement information when any of the measuring tools are active.

D As you drag the Distance tool's crosshair, a double arrow shows the distance you are measuring.

E The Distance tool leaves a special-purpose annotation—a *measurement markup*—on the page, displaying the double arrow and the distance value.

6.10 in

 **F** The Perimeter tool window displays the distance around a perimeter you define. Just click points on the edge of the area you are measuring.

G When you are finished, the Perimeter tool adds a measurement markup to the page. It indicates that the markup is an annotation by placing a flea-sized speech bubble next to the markup.

💬 ▾ **jrd**
9/23/10 5:13:15 PM

8.55 in

H Double-clicking the measurement markup displays a small window with the measurement value.

The Perimeter tool

The Perimeter tool measures the distance around a region on the page.

To measure the perimeter of a region:

1. Select the Perimeter tool in the Measurement palette **B**. The mouse pointer becomes a crosshair, and Acrobat displays the Measuring Info window **C**.

2. Click at the starting point of the path you want to measure.

3. Click successively on points around the perimeter of the area you want to measure.

   As you do so, Acrobat shows you the set of straight lines connecting your points as well as a running total of your distance so far **F**. This distance also appears in the Measuring Info window.

4. Click twice on the final point of your perimeter to let Acrobat know you're done.

   Acrobat freezes the values displayed in the Measuring Info window. It also adds the polygon you created to the page as a measurement markup, placing the world's tiniest speech bubble next to the polygon to let you know it really is an annotation **G**.

   TIP Having clicked around the perimeter of your region, you can double-click the resulting polygon annotation with the Hand tool, and Acrobat displays a comment window with the perimeter measurement **H**.

The Area tool

The Area tool works identically to the Perimeter tool except that it reports the area of the enclosed space you map out with your line segments.

To measure the area of a region:

1. Select the Area tool in the Measurement palette **B**.

   The mouse pointer becomes a crosshair, and the Measuring Info window opens **C**.

2. Click at the starting point of the region whose area you want to measure.

3. Click successively on points around the perimeter of the region.

   As you do so, Acrobat shows the set of straight lines connecting your points, as in **F**. Unlike with the Perimeter tool, there's no running total.

4. Click the starting point to close the region.

   The Measuring Info window displays the area of the region enclosed by your line segments. As before, Acrobat adds the polygon to the page as a measurement markup annotation **G**.

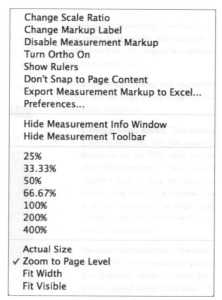

Change Scale Ratio
Change Markup Label
Disable Measurement Markup
Turn Ortho On
Show Rulers
Don't Snap to Page Content
Export Measurement Markup to Excel...
Preferences...

Hide Measurement Info Window
Hide Measurement Toolbar

25%
33.33%
50%
66.67%
100%
200%
400%

Actual Size
✓ Zoom to Page Level
Fit Width
Fit Visible

I Right-clicking (Control-clicking) the page with a measuring crosshair displays a context menu with useful settings.

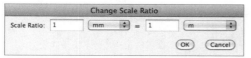

J The Change Scale Ratio dialog lets you set the scale for your distance, perimeter, and area measurements.

Measurement settings

Anytime the measuring crosshair is visible, you can right-click (Control-click) the page and get a context menu that lets you change the settings used by the measuring tools **I**.

There are several items you can select in this menu, but the ones I find to be the most generally useful include:

- **Change Scale Ratio.** This option presents you with a dialog that lets you specify how distances on the PDF page translate into real-life distances **J**. Thus, if your PDF file shows a map of your personal aircraft carrier, you can tell the measuring tools that each millimeter on the page represents one meter in real life and have the tools report the actual distance.

- **Disable Measurement Markup.** Sometimes I'm measuring distances or areas in a diagram but don't want the double arrows added to the PDF page. This menu item tells the measuring tools not to add the measurement markup comment to the page. The area or distance is reported in the Measuring Info window as usual, but no permanent mark is put on the page.

- **25%, 33.33%, Fit Page, and so on.** These options let you zoom in and out of the page while in the middle of a measurement. This can be extremely handy at times. I frequently find that I am two-thirds of the way through measuring a spectacularly fussy border and discover that the rest of the area falls beyond the border of the document window; with Acrobat X, I can zoom out and continue measuring.

continues on next page

TIP I almost always turn off the measurement markup. Generally, when I'm measuring the size of something on a PDF map or chart, I'm going to put that number into a spreadsheet or other document; I don't usually want the big double arrows and distance value drawn on top of the page contents.

TIP If you get an unwanted measurement markup on the page, you can easily remove it by clicking it with the Hand tool or Selection tool (both in the Favorites toolbar) and pressing the Delete key.

Saving and Printing Files

A document in your computer's memory is impermanent; turn off the power and it's gone. For your document to trot even a short distance down the sands of time, you need to be able to save it to disk and print it.

Acrobat lets you save your PDF documents to a remarkably wide variety of formats. If you need to convert a PDF file to a TIFF file or an EPS file, just select one of those formats when you save the file.

When you print a document, Acrobat gives you a lot of control over the details of how your document is placed on paper. You can even make a booklet out of your PDF file directly from Acrobat.

In this chapter, you'll learn how to use all of Acrobat's file saving, conversion, and printing capabilities.

In This Chapter

Saving a PDF File

Many of the tasks in this book describe how to modify the documents you're working with; commenting, touching up text, and adding links all change the file. To make these changes permanent, you must save the file back to your hard disk.

Acrobat does this the same way as most other applications.

To save a document to disk:

Do one of the following:

- Choose File > Save.
- Click the Save button in the Quick Tools toolbar **A**.

Acrobat saves the PDF file onto your hard disk with its existing name.

To save a document with a new name:

1. Choose File > Save As > PDF.

   Acrobat presents you with a standard Save As dialog **B**.

2. Navigate to the folder on your disk in which you want to save the file.

3. Type a new name for your document into the File Name field.

4. Click Save.

   Acrobat saves your file in the location you specified.

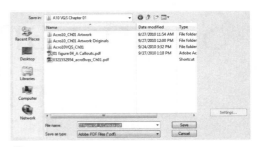

A The Quick Tools toolbar contains a Save File tool that lets you save your document to a PDF file or export to a different format.

B When you choose a selection from the File > Save As submenu, a standard Save As dialog opens.

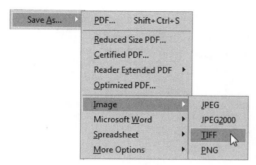

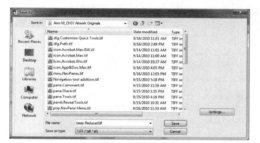

A In Acrobat X, you export to another file format by simply saving to that format with the Save As submenu.

B Acrobat X uses the standard Mac and Windows Save As dialog with a Settings button added.

Exporting to Other Formats

Acrobat can save a PDF document to a variety of other formats, such as TIFF, PNG, and EPS. You do this by choosing the desired file format from the File > Save As submenu **A**.

If you carefully examine the submenu in the figure, you'll see that you can also save your file as various flavors of specialized PDF, as well. We'll talk about these in some detail later in the book.

To save a file to a different format:

1. Choose your file format in the File > Save As submenu.

   Acrobat presents you with a standard Save As dialog **B**.

continues on next page

Flavors of PDF

Not only can you export your PDF files to TIFF and the like, you can also convert them to other PDF file types. These are still PDF files, just modified, optimized, or otherwise changed for some purpose.

We'll talk about most of these in some detail later, but for now, the choices include:

- **Reduced Size PDF.** The PDF file has a set of automated changes applied to it that reduces the file size. We'll talk about this later in this chapter.

- **Certified PDF.** The file has a signature key embedded in it that certifies the file actually came from you. We'll talk about this in Chapter 16.

- **Reader Extended PDF.** This allows users of Adobe Reader 9 and earlier to add comments to the file. (Acrobat X can do this without having to specially set up the file.)

- **Optimized PDF.** This is similar to Reduced Size PDF but gives you some control over the process. As is often the case, the default settings give perfectly good results.

2. If you want to change the details of how the file is converted, click the Settings button.

A Settings dialog opens for the file format you selected 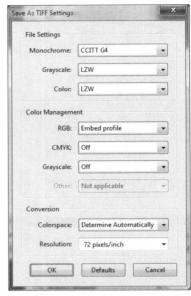.

3. Make whatever changes you wish to the settings and click OK to return to the Save As dialog. You can usually use the defaults with no problems. (See the sidebar "TIFF and EPS Options.")

4. Navigate to the folder on your disk in which you want to save your file.

5. Click Save.

Acrobat saves your document in the file format you specified.

TIP In the Save As dialog, you can change your mind about the file format to which you want to export your file. Simply pick the format you want from the Save as type drop-down menu beneath the File name field **D**.

C Each output file format has a set of controls that dictate the details of the conversion.

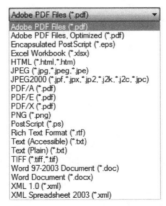

D The Save dialog's Save as type menu lets you change your mind about what conversion you want to perform.

TIFF and EPS Options

Of all the file types to which Acrobat can convert PDF, two are routinely useful for most people: TIFF and EPS. These are widely used as illustration formats by high-end page-layout and graphics software such as Adobe InDesign and Adobe Photoshop.

Most of Acrobat's defaults for these formats' file-type settings are perfectly good. For each of them, however, you should change a couple of these settings. These settings are sticky; once you change them, Acrobat will use the new values until you change them again.

TIFF settings: **C**

- Change the resolution (at the bottom of the dialog) to match that of the device on which the illustration will be printed or displayed:
  - ▸ For a printed document, choose 300 dpi for laser printers or 1200 dpi for high-resolution printers.
  - ▸ For onscreen presentations, choose 72 dpi.

EPS general settings: **E**

- Choose ASCII to ensure compatibility with all networks.

- Choose Embedded Fonts to eliminate problems with missing fonts.

- Select Convert TrueType to Type 1 to eliminate completely the rare problems associated with TrueType fonts.

- Select Include Preview so that importing applications can more easily work with the file.

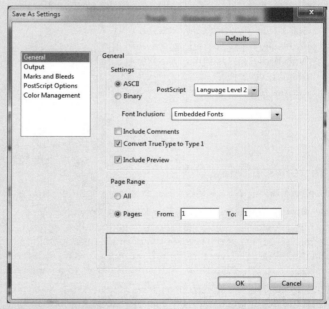

E The EPS settings shown here always work well.

Export file types

Acrobat can export PDF files to a variety of other file types from the File > Save As submenu. Unfortunately, in most cases the conversion changes the document's appearance: items move around, fonts change, illustrations come out pixelated, and other problems occur. The conversions work best for simple documents.

That said, you may need to save a PDF file to some of these formats. Following is a list of the file types to which Acrobat converts most successfully and the purpose of each.

- **Adobe PDF Files (vector).** Acrobat's default file format. Acrobat saves the PDF file as is.

- **Adobe PDF Files, Optimized (vector).** Still a PDF file, but compressed and internally reorganized for viewing in a Web browser. Use this type if you'll be posting your PDF file on the Web for people to read online.

Vector vs. Bitmap

Each export file type is identified as either vector or bitmap.

Vector files retain their quality regardless of the display or printing device. In particular, edges never become jagged regardless of the zoom level or the printer's resolution (dpi). On the other hand, vector files are prone to missing fonts and images, and other problems that are often hard to diagnose.

Bitmap export files consist of a series of full-page images of all the document's pages. This makes them immune to missing fonts and other problems to which vector formats are prone. However, bitmap files are inherently tied to a device resolution. If the bitmap is intended for a device of one resolution and you print it on a device of another resolution, the results may look bad **ⓕ**.

You should use vector file types unless you have consistent problems with fonts or other hard-to-fix printing problems.

ⓕ Vector file images (top) always look smooth. Bitmap file images (bottom) become jagged if you zoom in on them.

Piranha
Piranha
Piranha

G Here is some PDF text exported to (from top to bottom) EPS, TIFF, and JPEG. The JPEG artifacts appear somewhat exaggerated because the text was created with the non-default Low Quality setting.

- **Encapsulated PostScript (vector).** A file format used for illustrations in high-end graphics and page-layout software. EPS is usually your most dependable choice if the PDF file will be used as an illustration **G**.

- **Excel Workbook.** Saves to a spreadsheet and attempts to recognize tables in the PDF file and convert them to cells in the resulting spreadsheet file. This is new to Acrobat X, by the way. It's extremely useful if you receive spreadsheets in PDF format from other people and want to do your own analysis of the data, not just admire the numbers.

- **JPEG (bitmap).** A compact bitmap format widely used for images, including digital photography. It's useful only for photographs; it's particularly bad for general PDF files, because line art and text usually become surrounded by a halo of artifacts, as in the bottom text in **G**.

- **PDF/A (vector).** A PDF file that is organized so it is useful for long-term archiving of a document. If you are creating a PDF file that must still be readable 20 years from now, this is the recommended format.

- **PDF/E (vector).** A PDF file that has a variety of information embedded in it so it is useful for engineering documents. Use this if the document consists of construction plans or other engineering content.

- **PDF/X (vector).** A PDF file that is internally organized for use in prepress. Select this if you will send the PDF file to a print shop for high-quality, professional print.

continues on next page

- **Rich Text Format (vector).** A format that's commonly understood by a wide range of applications, although conversion to it isn't always successful. If you want to convert your PDF file into a word-processing document, this is worth trying.

- **Text (Accessible).** A format that extracts the text from the PDF file and attempts to preserve threading and other internal information that makes it easier to use the text with Braille readers. This information must have been put into the PDF file by the creator and is usually absent.

- **Text (Plain).** A format that extracts the text in the PDF file, removing all formatting information and illustrations. The text may come out scrambled if it's formatted in multiple columns.

- **TIFF (bitmap).** The best format if you need to convert your PDF pages to a series of images. The format is reasonably compact, and text and line art look much better than in JPEG .

- **Word Document.** Save the document in Microsoft Word format. Adobe has put a lot of effort into improving the quality of Acrobat's export to Microsoft Word. It is noticeably better, but don't be surprised if you get misplaced text and illustrations, and dramatic font changes. Still, Adobe does an excellent job of handling a very difficult conversion problem.

Letter.pdf

Letter_Page_4.tiff
Letter_Page_3.tiff
Letter_Page_2.tiff
Letter_Page_1.tiff

H When you save a PDF file to a bitmap format, such as JPEG or TIFF, Acrobat creates an image file for each page.

TIP If you need to export your pages as illustrations in page-layout or other software, use either EPS or TIFF. EPS is the better choice generally, but if you're having trouble with fonts in the EPS file, go back and resave the PDF file as a TIFF. Keep in mind that because it's a bitmap, the TIFF illustration will become ugly if you scale it.

TIP Despite the preceding tip, most high-end page-layout programs (and just about all programs on the Mac) can use PDF files directly as illustrations without converting them to other formats; *that's* the best choice.

TIP If you save a multipage PDF file in one of the bitmap formats, such as JPEG or TIFF, Acrobat creates one bitmap file per page **H**.

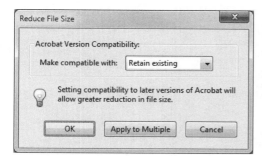

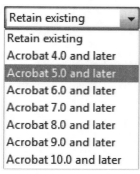

A The Reduce File Size dialog lets you choose the earliest version of Acrobat with which your file must be compatible.

B Select the earliest version of Acrobat that your readers might own.

Minimizing File Size

Once you've saved your document, you can often reduce its size using an Acrobat feature that looks through the PDF file and makes some internal changes. This process entails rearranging the structure of the document, optimizing image compression, and storing repeated graphics in a more efficient form.

You should always use this feature with PDF files you'll be distributing electronically. It often makes little difference, but sometimes it results in an impressive reduction in file size.

To reduce the size of a PDF file:

1. With your document open, choose File > Save As > Reduced Size PDF. The Reduce File Size dialog opens **A**.

2. From the Acrobat Version Compatibility pop-up menu, choose the earliest version of Acrobat with which your file must remain compatible **B**.

   Choosing later versions of Acrobat may result in a smaller file, but it will also prevent people from reading the file if they haven't upgraded their version of Acrobat. The default value is Retain Existing; this means the new file should have the same Acrobat compatibility as the original.

3. Click OK.

   The Save As dialog opens.

4. Provide a name for the new, slimmed-down file, and click OK.

   After a few moments, Acrobat saves the reduced file with the new name.

   continues on next page

TIP You can save the reduced file with the same name as the original if you'd like. Doing so replaces the original file.

TIP For the optimum trade-off between small file size and broad compatibility, I recommend choosing Acrobat 5 for your compatibility setting. This presumes your file won't be read with an electronic book reader or other device that requires specialized internal information.

TIP If you click the Apply to Multiple button in the Reduce File Size dialog, Acrobat presents you with another dialog that lets you select several PDF files to reduce all at once **C**.

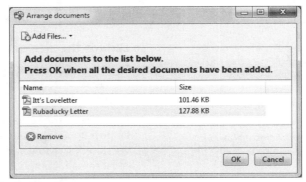

C Acrobat can reduce the size of several files at once, applying the settings you selected in the Reduce File Size dialog **A**.

Printing a Document

Visions of the paperless office notwithstanding, PDF is routinely used to distribute printed documents. After you open a PDF file and peruse it onscreen, you may want to print it for reading at your leisure.

To print a PDF document:

1. Choose File > Print, or click the Print tool in the Quick Tools toolbar.

   Acrobat presents you with the Print dialog **A**.

2. Choose the options you want.

   In most cases, it's fine to accept the default values for these controls. Most of the controls are at least occasionally important, however, and we'll discuss them next.

3. Click OK.

   Acrobat prints your document.

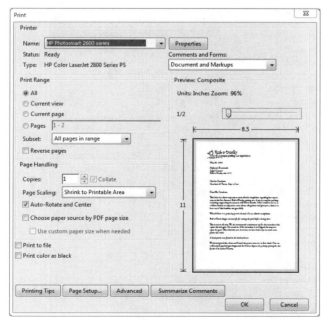

A The Print dialog lets you choose from a wide range of options. In most cases, the default values work fine.

Miscellaneous settings

- **Print to File (Windows).** This is a standard Windows check box that tells Acrobat to send the printer code to a file rather than to the printer. This option is occasionally used in professional printing to capture PostScript code for the document.

- **Print Color As Black (Windows).** This option converts colors to black. It may be useful if you're printing diagrams with a lot of thin, light-colored lines.

- **Printing Tips.** If you're connected to the Internet, clicking this button launches your Web browser and takes you to troubleshooting tips in Adobe's Knowledgebase.

TIP Don't ignore the preview picture in the Print dialog **B**. A quick examination of this picture can tell you whether your document will print as you expect.

TIP The slider control above the preview picture in the Print dialog lets you step through the pages in your document.

TIP Selecting the Collate check box in the Print dialog **A** can significantly slow your printing speed, because Acrobat must resend the printing code for each copy of each page in your document. I suggest you routinely leave it deselected and collate by hand. (This warning doesn't apply if you actually have a collator attached to your printer.)

TIP If the size and position of items on your printed page seem off by a small amount, check to make sure you didn't print the document with **Shrink to Printable Area** selected in the Page Scaling menu **C**. This option may reduce the size of the page contents by a few percent. None is usually a better choice.

TIP The Fit to Printable Area scale selection **C** is for when your document is being clipped at the edges. This option scales down the PDF page so it all fits within the printer's built-in borders.

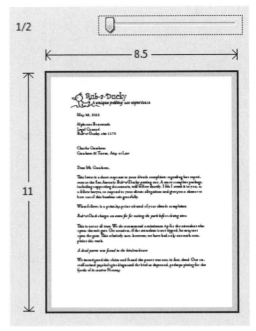

B The preview picture in the Print dialog shows you how your printed pages will look. The slider above the picture lets you move among the pages

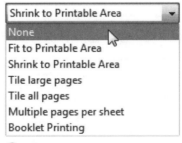

C The Shrink to Printable Area and the Fit to Printable Area settings may change the size of your page contents.

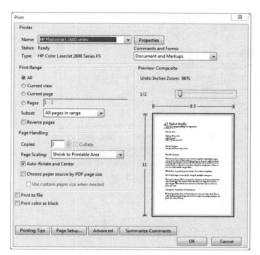

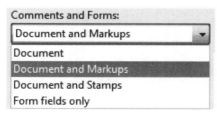

A The Print dialog allows you remarkable control over the printing of your PDF file.

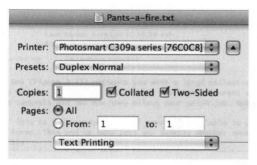

B The Macintosh Print dialog has Mac standard controls at the top, but otherwise has the same Acrobat-specific controls as in Windows.

Comments and Forms:

Document and Markups ▼

Document
Document and Markups
Document and Stamps
Form fields only

C The Comments and Forms pop-up menu lets you decide whether to print the contents of annotations and form fields.

Print Options

The Print dialog **A** presents you with a large collection of choices that determine the details of how your document prints. Although you can usually accept the default values for these options, sometimes you'll need to change them.

The Macintosh and Windows versions of this dialog look different superficially, but the Acrobat-specific controls are entirely identical. The dialogs differ only in the controls that are standard to the two environments' Print dialogs. For example, the top of the Macintosh version of this dialog **B** has pop-up menus for Presets and Option categories, whereas Windows has printer status text and a Properties button.

Let's look at the controls and see how they affect your print job. Note that the dialog's preview always reflects the controls' current settings.

Printer controls

- **Printer Name.** This is the standard menu of printers available to your computer. Choose the printer you want to use.

- **Comments and Forms.** This pop-up menu lets you specify whether annotations and form field contents (generically called markups in Acrobat) should be printed along with the document pages **C**.

Print-range controls

- **All, Current View, Current Page, Pages.** These four radio buttons choose the pages within your document that you want to print. They're self-explanatory, with one possible exception: The Pages text field  accepts a hyphen to indicate a contiguous range of pages, and commas to separate discontiguous pages. Thus, "1-4" prints pages 1 through 4, and "1, 4, 7" prints pages 1, 4, and 7.

- **Subset.** This pop-up menu lets you choose to print even pages, odd pages, or both ⓔ. It's useful for manually printing duplex documents.

- **Reverse Pages.** Acrobat prints the pages in reverse order. This is convenient if your printer delivers its pages faceup; the stack of output ends up in the correct order.

Page-handling controls

- **Copies.** Specifies the number of copies you want of each page.

- **Collate.** If you print multiple copies of a document, the pages are collated.

- **Page Scaling.** This menu lets you resize the document pages in a variety of ways ⓕ. The most routinely useful selections are as follows:

  - The None option prints the document in its native size; this is usually what you want.

ⓓ The Pages field accepts hyphens to indicate a contiguous range of pages, and commas to separate individual pages.

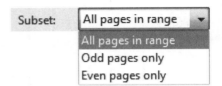

ⓔ Choose to print odd, even, or all pages within your specified range.

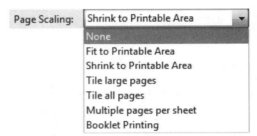

ⓕ The Page Scaling menu tells Acrobat to scale the document page.

 Fit to Printable Area scales the page up or down until it exactly fits within the current paper area.

 Autorotate and Center moves the contents of the document page so they're centered on the paper.

- ▸ Fit to Printable Area shrinks or expands the page so it fits within the printer's native printable area. This makes the document page as large as it can be without losing information off the edges of the paper .

- ▸ Shrink to Printable Area shrinks the page so it fits within the printer's native printable area. This ensures that items near the edges of your pages (such as headers and footers) print successfully.

We'll look at other selections in this menu later in this chapter.

- ■ **Autorotate and Center.** This option repositions the page so it's centered on the paper . It may also rotate the page if Acrobat thinks it's necessary (usually not). This may be useful if you want to center a small document page on a large piece of paper.

- ■ **Choose Paper Source by PDF Page Size (Windows).** This option overrides the printer's default paper size and uses each page's paper size as specified in the PDF file. It's useful if you are printing a document whose pages vary in size on a printer with multiple paper trays; Acrobat selects the paper from whichever tray most closely matches the page's size.

Printing multiple pages per sheet

You'll sometimes want to print two or more pages of your document on each piece of paper. Acrobat's Print dialog lets you do this easily.

To print multiple pages on each printed page:

1. Choose File > Print.

   The Print dialog opens.

2. In the Page Scaling pop-up menu, choose Multiple Pages per Sheet **I**.

   Acrobat displays additional controls beneath the Page Scaling pop-up menu. In addition, the Print dialog's preview reflects the multiple pages **J**.

3. From the Pages per Sheet menu, choose the number of pages you want on each sheet of paper.

   As always, the preview picture shows the change.

4. Click OK.

   Acrobat prints your document with the specified number of pages on each sheet of paper.

TIP If you choose Custom from the Pages per Sheet pop-up menu, you can specify how many pages you want across and down each sheet **K**.

TIP I often make a reference page with thumbnails of all of my document's pages by printing with 16 pages per sheet. The text is unreadable, but it provides me with a usable overview of my document's layout.

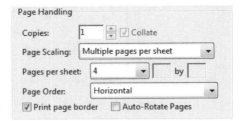

I When you choose Multiple Pages per Sheet from the Page Scaling menu, Acrobat displays additional controls.

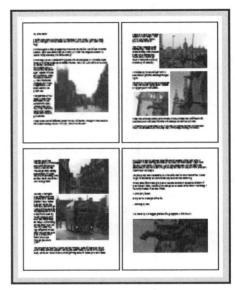

J The preview picture in the Print dialog reflects the number of pages you're printing on each sheet of paper.

K If you choose Custom from the Pages per Sheet menu, you can specify how many pages you want across and down each sheet.

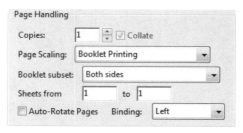

L To turn a four-page document into a booklet, Acrobat prints pages 4 and 1 on one side of the paper and pages 2 and 3 on the other.

M Fold the paper to make your booklet. For longer documents, stack the paper and staple the stack in the middle before folding.

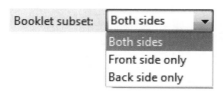

N When you choose Booklet Printing, Acrobat displays additional controls that let you specify the details.

O Printing the front and back sides separately allows you to print a booklet on a printer that doesn't print double-sided.

Printing a booklet

Sometimes, when proofing a document, it's useful to turn a PDF file into a booklet. When you choose this feature, Acrobat prints your document two pages per sheet of paper, double-sided, reordering the pages as needed to make a booklet **L** and **M**.

To print a document as a booklet:

1. Choose File > Print.

   Acrobat displays the Print dialog.

2. In the Page Scaling pop-up menu, choose Booklet Printing.

   Acrobat displays additional controls beneath the Page Scaling pop-up menu **N**. As always, the preview reflects the new arrangement of the pages.

3. From the Booklet Subset pop-up menu, choose Front Side Only or Back Side Only if you want to print only one side of each sheet of paper **O**.

   These options let you print a booklet on a printer that can't print double-sided. You can print the front sides of all the pages, put the paper back into the printer, and then print the back sides.

continues on next page

4. In the "Sheets from ... to" fields, type the beginning and end of the range of paper sheets you want to print.

   Confusingly, entering a zero in both of these fields means "print all the sheets." This is what you'll usually want.

5. In the Binding pop-up menu, specify whether the booklet will be bound on the left or the right.

6. Click OK.

   Acrobat prints your document as a booklet.

TIP The ability to print a booklet is surprisingly handy. I often take a document I'm working on and, before sending it to the print shop, print it with Booklet Printing, stack the resulting pages, and ram a staple through its heart. Immediately, I can see how it feels to page through my document on physical paper.

Printing Terminology

Here are some terms you may encounter when reading about printing:

- **Duplex.** Printing on both sides of a sheet of paper.

- **Simplex.** Printing on only one side of each sheet of paper.

- **2-up, 3-up,** and so on. Printing more than one page on each sheet. The number is the number of pages per sheet.

- **Imposition.** Rearranging pages for printing a book. The verb is *impose*.

Using these terms, you can say that to make a booklet, your document is printed 2-up, duplex, imposed.

Creating PDF Files

PDF is arguably the best file format for storing and distributing documents. It's compact, it supports a wide variety of content (including text, images, line art, and multimedia), and you can use it for free without incurring licensing fees. However, all this capability is useless unless you can conveniently create PDF files. This is the topic we address in this chapter.

When you install Acrobat, you also install features into your computer system that make it easy and quick to generate PDF files from within virtually any Macintosh or Windows application. Furthermore, Acrobat has many powerful features that let you create PDF files: you can convert many common file types to PDF, scan paper documents directly into PDF, convert Web pages to PDF files, and combine several PDF files into a single document.

In this chapter, you learn how to do all of these tasks.

In This Chapter

Printing to a PDF File

Acrobat makes it easy to create PDF files from any application—spreadsheet, database, image editing, word processor—by simply printing to a PDF file. If you can print your document, you can convert it to PDF.

However, the details are a bit different between the Macintosh and Windows.

Printing to Adobe PDF in Windows

When you install the Windows version of Acrobat X, you also install onto your computer system a virtual printer called Adobe PDF. When you print to this "printer," it converts the document being printed into a PDF file rather than producing sheets of paper.

To print to a PDF file in Windows:

1. Choose File > Print in your application.

   The standard Windows Print dialog opens .

2. In the Printer pop-up menu, choose Adobe PDF.

3. Click Print.

   A standard Save File dialog opens.

4. Type a name for your PDF file.

5. Click OK.

   After a short while, you will see a newly created PDF file on your disk.

> **TIP** If you click the Properties button that's visible in , you will be presented with some settings that determine the characteristics of the new PDF file **B**. The default settings, shown here, are reasonable.

A Acrobat installs onto your system a virtual printer named Adobe PDF. When printed to, this printer creates a PDF file.

B The Adobe PDF virtual printer has a collection of settings that affect how it works. The default values work well.

PDF ▾

Save as PDF...
Save as PostScript...
Fax PDF...

Mail PDF
Save as Adobe PDF
Save as PDF-X
Save PDF to Aperture
Save PDF to folder as JPEG
Save PDF to folder as TIFF
Save PDF to iPhoto

Edit Menu...

Ⓒ Printing to a PDF file is built into Macintosh OS X. This PDF drop-down menu is at the bottom of the standard Mac Print dialog and is available in every application.

Printing to Adobe PDF on the Macintosh

You don't actually need Acrobat to either create or view PDF files on a Macintosh. Because the Mac's internal drawing language is based on PDF, the Mac can display and create PDF files on its own. However, Adobe has a lot more experience working with PDF (they invented it, after all), and Acrobat reflects this by creating PDF files that much more completely support all of PDF's capabilities: all the annotation types, the form fields, and so on.

In the past, Acrobat installed an Adobe PDF printer driver on the Mac, as it does in Windows. However, Acrobat X installs itself into the standard Mac printing mechanism, making for a more Mac-like experience.

Every Print dialog on the Macintosh has a PDF drop-down menu that offers a set of useful print-to-PDF functions **Ⓒ**. Acrobat X adds to this menu a Print to Adobe PDF item; when you select this, the document is printed to a PDF file using Adobe PDF rather than Apple's built-in PDF generator.

To print to Adobe PDF on the Macintosh:

1. Choose File > Print in your application. The standard Mac Print dialog opens.

2. In the PDF drop-down menu, choose Save as Adobe PDF 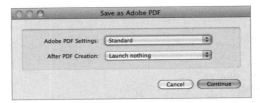.

   You are presented with the Save as Adobe PDF dialog .

3. Choose the settings you wish in the dialog.

   The Settings pop-up menu lets you choose parameters appropriate to common document types ; Standard will work fine in most cases. The After PDF Creation menu gives you the option of opening the new PDF file in Acrobat .

4. Click Continue.

   A standard Save dialog opens.

5. Type a name for your PDF file.

6. Click OK.

   After a short while, you will see a newly created PDF file on your disk.

D When you print a document to Adobe PDF on a Mac, you are presented with the Save as Adobe PDF dialog.

E The Settings pop-up menu lets you specify the purpose of the PDF file you are creating.

F You can also specify whether the newly created PDF file should be automatically opened in Acrobat.

Using PDFMaker in Microsoft Office (Windows)

The Windows version of Acrobat X automatically installs a set of tools into the Microsoft Office suite of software **A**. These tools are known collectively as PDFMaker.

The appearance and abilities of PDFMaker vary depending on your version of Office and which Office component you are working with. In Microsoft Word 2010, it installs tools that let you do the following:

- Create a PDF file of the current document.

- Email the current document as a PDF file to an address of your choice.

- Do a Word mail merge and save the result as a PDF file.

- Send the current document to a list of people so they can comment on it.

- Convert the document to PDF and open it in Acrobat for comment.

The Create PDF and Email PDF functions are available in all versions of Office, making it very simple to convert Word, Excel, and other Office documents to PDF.

The instructions on the next page are for Office 2010. Earlier versions of Office have the same functions, but they may reside in a PDFMaker toolbar rather than an Acrobat "ribbon."

A Acrobat X installs PDFMaker, a set of PDF-related controls, into the Microsoft Office applications.

To create a PDF file in an Office application:

1. With your Office document active, select the Acrobat ribbon 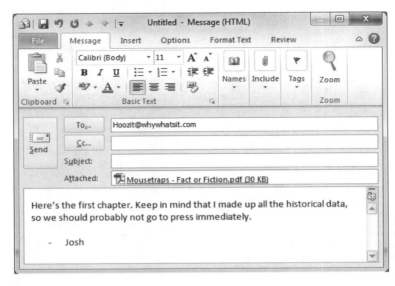.

2. Click the Create PDF button.

   Office presents you with the standard Save dialog.

3. Specify a name and location for your PDF file.

4. Click OK.

Acrobat creates the PDF file, displaying a progress bar while it works.

TIP PDFMaker uses the Adobe PDF virtual printer behind the scenes, so don't be alarmed if your Office application seems to be printing in the background when you use this toolbar.

TIP If you Mac users are feeling left out because the Mac version of Microsoft Office doesn't have a PDFMaker, you don't need it. PDFMaker isn't relevant to the Mac, because nearly all of its functions are available in the standard Mac Print dialog. (Reread the earlier section "Printing to a PDF File.")

To email an Office document as a PDF file:

1. With the Acrobat ribbon active **A**, click the Create and Attach to Email button.

   The standard Save dialog opens.

2. Specify a name and location for your PDF file.

3. Click OK.

   Acrobat creates the PDF file, displaying a progress bar while it works.

   When it's finished, PDFMaker launches your email client software and opens a blank email window with the new PDF file already attached **B**.

4. Fill out the destination address and subject in your email client.

5. Click your email client's Send button.

TIP Depending on your email client, PDF-Maker may ask you for an email address and subject, and send the PDF file directly without launching your email client.

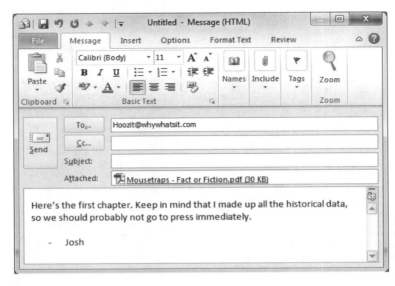

B The Create and Attach to Email tool launches your email client and opens a blank message that has the new PDF file attached to it.

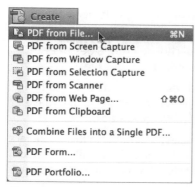

A The Create menu on the Quick Tools toolbar lets you create a PDF file from a variety of sources.

B Acrobat X's Preferences let you specify the details of how it converts the various file formats to PDF.

Conversion File Types

Acrobat X can convert the following types of files to PDF:

- 3D
- BMP
- GIF
- HTML
- InDesign
- JPEG
- JPEG2000

- Multimedia
- PCX
- PICT
- PNG
- PostScript/EPS
- Text
- TIFF

This list encompasses the most common graphic, design, and image formats.

Converting Images and Other Files to PDF

Acrobat X can convert a variety of file types to PDF and then open them in a document window. The list of supported file types includes all the common vector and image formats (see the sidebar "Conversion File Types").

Converting these files to PDF is remarkably easy; you just open the file in Acrobat.

To convert a file to PDF:

1. In the Quick Tools toolbar, click the Create button and choose PDF from File in the drop-down menu **A**.

   Acrobat presents you with a standard pick-a-file dialog.

2. Choose the file that you want to convert to PDF.

   This can be an image file, a Word document, or any other file type that Acrobat knows how to convert.

   Acrobat converts the file to PDF and opens it in a new document window.

3. If you want to save the document on your disk, choose File > Save As.

TIP If you are avoiding toolbars for some reason, you can also access these conversions by choosing from the File > Create submenu.

TIP Acrobat's Preferences include a large collection of controls that determine how it converts files to PDF. The default values for these controls are sensible and should generally be left as is. However, as you gain experience you may find it interesting to look at them. On the Mac choose Acrobat > Preferences, or in Windows choose Edit > Preferences, to access the Convert to PDF options **B**.

Scanning Directly to PDF

Using Acrobat, you can scan paper documents directly to a PDF file. Acrobat can operate any scanner with a TWAIN driver or a Windows Image Acquisition (WIA) driver. Most scanners install on a computer with one or both of these drivers.

Remember that if you scan a text document, the result is a picture of the text, not the text itself; the resulting document isn't searchable. Acrobat can use Optical Character Recognition (OCR) technology to convert the scanned text to real text; you'll learn how to do this in Chapter 17.

To scan a page directly to PDF:

1. On the Quick Tools toolbar, click the Create button and choose PDF from Scanner from the drop-down menu **A**. The Acrobat Scan dialog opens **B**.

2. From the Scanner pop-up menu, choose the scanner you want to use. This menu lists all the TWAIN and WIA scanners visible to your computer.

3. Choose the settings for the scan:

   ▸ If your scanner can do double-sided scans, choose Front Sides or Both Sides from the Sides menu.

   ▸ If you want to convert scanned text to searchable text, select the Make Searchable check box.

   The remaining controls in this dialog are best left at their default settings. Check Acrobat Help for a description of them.

4. Click Scan.

   Acrobat scans your document and opens the resulting file in a new PDF document window.

5. Choose File > Save As to save your new PDF file to your disk.

> **TIP** You can select the Append radio button in the Acrobat Scan dialog to add your scanned page to the end of an existing PDF file. I use this sometimes when scanning receipts that need to be added to a PDF-format invoice.

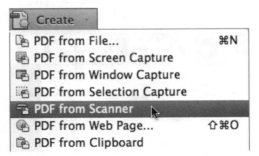

A The Quick Tools toolbar lets you scan a paper document directly to PDF.

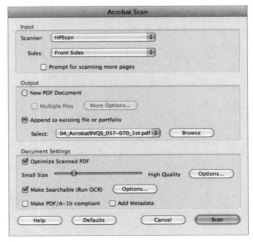

B The Acrobat Scan dialog lets you control how your scanned document is converted to PDF.

A The Create PDF from Web Page dialog lets you specify the URL of a Web page you want to convert to PDF.

B If you click the Capture Multiple Levels button, you get additional controls that limit the scope of the Web page conversion.

Converting Web Pages to PDF

Acrobat can convert a Web page or an entire Web site into a single PDF file. The result is a self-contained PDF version of the original Web page, with all images and graphics intact and with functioning links.

I use this feature to convert online manuals and other documentation into a PDF file that I can keep, read, and search offline.

To convert a single Web page to PDF:

1. On the Quick Tools toolbar, choose Create > PDF from Web Page.

   Acrobat presents you with the Create PDF from Web Page dialog **A**.

2. In the URL field, type the complete Web address of the Web page you want to convert to PDF.

3. If you want to capture part of the entire Web *site* (that is, not just a single Web page), click the Capture Multiple Levels button, which reveals some additional controls **B**:

   ▸ In the Get Only field, type the depth to which you want to convert the site. (See the sidebar "Web Site Conversion Settings.")

   ▸ Select both "Stay on same path" and "Stay on same server."

   continues on next page

4. Click Create.

Acrobat displays the Download Status dialog , showing you how the conversion is progressing.

When the conversion is finished, Acrobat displays the converted Web page or site in a document window. Note that there will be some differences in the text and graphics when they are converted. These changes are usually comparable to how a page's appearance changes from one Web browser to another.

C As Acrobat converts the Web site to PDF, it shows you how the conversion is progressing.

Web Site Conversion Settings

The controls in the Create PDF from Web Page dialog **B** have the critical purpose of limiting the scope of your Web capture. At the extreme, they keep you from inadvertently trying to convert the entire World Wide Web into a single (large!) PDF file.

- **Get only n level(s).** Here you specify the extent to which Acrobat should grab Web pages that are the target of links on your selected Web page. A value of 1 says to get only the Web page whose address you have specified. A value of 2 says to get that Web page and any pages linked to by that page. A value of 3 additionally captures pages linked to by *those* pages, and so forth. Keep this number small. *Very* small. The larger the number of levels you specify, the exponentially longer the conversion will take.

- **Get entire site.** As it says, this option converts the entire site to PDF. I strongly recommend against selecting this option, because it can take an amazingly long time.

- **Stay on same path.** Like all files, the HTML files that make up a Web site reside in a directory on a hard disk—in this case, the Web server's disk. This option prevents Acrobat from following links that reside outside the target Web page's location or its subdirectories. I recommend choosing this option.

- **Stay on same server.** Acrobat won't follow links off your target page's server. I strongly recommend this option. Otherwise, for example, if the page you request has links to its sponsors, you may find yourself trying to convert all of Microsoft's Web site to a PDF file.

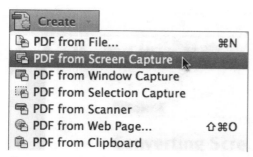

Ⓐ On the Macintosh, Acrobat can capture parts of your computer screen and convert the image to PDF.

Ⓑ When you capture a window, the mouse pointer changes to a camera. Cute.

Converting Screen Shots to PDF

PDF from Screen Capture is a Macintosh-only feature. When it's selected, Acrobat lets you capture the contents of a window, a region, or an entire screen to a PDF file. This is convenient for people who write computer documentation.

The directions below all send you to the Create button in the Quick Tools toolbar; keep in mind that these commands are also available in the File > Create submenu.

To capture an entire screen to PDF:

1. In the Quick Tools toolbar, choose Create > PDF from Screen Capture **Ⓐ**.

    After a moment, Acrobat presents you with a document window containing an image of the entire screen.

2. Choose File > Save As to save this file to disk.

To capture a window to PDF:

1. In the Quick Tools toolbar, choose Create > PDF from Window Capture.

    The mouse pointer changes to a camera **Ⓑ**. As the pointer moves over the windows open on the screen, the current window turns blue.

2. Click the window whose contents you want to capture.

    A document opens, containing an image of the window you clicked.

3. Choose File > Save As to save this file to disk.

To capture a region of the desktop to PDF:

1. In the Quick Tools toolbar, choose Create > PDF from Selection Capture.

   The pointer changes to a crosshair.

2. Click and drag a rectangular marquee around the area you want to capture. Acrobat uses a nonstandard marquee with this tool: You drag out a light gray area on the screen .

   Acrobat presents you with a document containing the contents of the region you enclosed .

3. Choose File > Save As to save this file to disk.

C When capturing a part of the screen, you drag out a light gray rectangle that indicates the capture area.

D The area of the screen you selected turns into a PDF image.

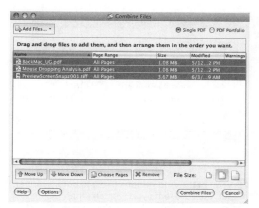

(A) The Combine Files dialog lets you choose several files of any type that you want to merge.

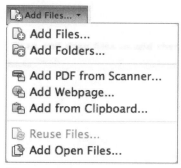

(B) You can combine files of any type, folders of files, data direct from a scanner, Web pages slurped up off the Web, or the contents of the clipboard into a single PDF file.

Merging PDF Files

Acrobat can combine multiple files into a single PDF file. The component files can be PDF files, TIFF files, EPS files, or files of any format that Acrobat can convert to PDF. This is extremely useful for combining, say, all the files associated with an invoice—the invoice itself, an expense report, scanned receipts, justifications for your hourly rate, letters from your lawyer—into a single file you can email.

To merge several PDF files into a single PDF file:

1. In the Quick Tools toolbar, choose Create > Combine Files into a Single PDF.

   The Combine Files dialog opens **(A)**. This dialog lets you choose a list of files to combine.

2. Choose one of the following from the Add Files drop-down menu **(B)**:

   ▸ **Add Files** lets you add individual files to the list.

   ▸ **Add Folders** lets you choose a folder, all of whose convertible contents will be added to the list.

   ▸ **Add PDF from Scanner** and **Add Webpage** run the scanner and Web conversion features, and then add the resulting PDF file to the list.

   ▸ **Add from Clipboard** converts the contents of the clipboard to a PDF file and adds the result to the list.

   ▸ **Reuse Files** lets you choose files inside a PDF portfolio.

   ▸ **Add Open Files** allows you to choose among all open files.

continues on next page

No matter which option you choose, Acrobat displays an Open dialog appropriate to the task 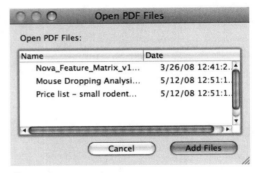.

3. Repeat step 2 as often as needed, adding items to the list, until your list is complete.

   The list of files currently selected is displayed in the Combine Multiple Files dialog. You can click the Move Up and Move Down arrows beneath the list to alter the files' order.

4. Select the Single PDF radio button in the upper-right corner of the Combine Multiple Files dialog.

   We'll discuss the alternative, PDF Portfolio, in Chapter 6.

5. Click Combine Files.

   Acrobat merges the files together and displays a standard Save dialog.

6. Specify a name for the new, merged PDF file and click OK.

   Acrobat saves the new PDF file.

C Each of the Add options (files, folders, scanner output, etc.) presents you with an Open dialog appropriate to that task. This dialog is what you see when you add files to the list.

TIP In **A**, you see three File Size icons in the lower-right corner of the dialog; they let you choose a qualitative file size (small, medium, or large). These options mostly affect how aggressively images in your document are compressed. Clicking the "small" icon results in the greatest compression. Unfortunately, this compression also reduces the images' quality, so you want to treat these icons with a little caution. When in doubt, choose the "medium" icon.

Note that if there are no images in your PDF files, you probably won't see much difference among these options.

TIP Acrobat creates bookmarks in the merged file that take you to the start of each of the original documents. (See Chapter 2 for a reminder of how to use bookmarks.)

Sharing Files with Acrobat.com

No computer is an island these days. The PDF files that you create will almost certainly be shared with someone else.

To do this, you need access to a server that lets you distribute your document. Email requires a mail server to collect and distribute your email; file sharing requires a filer server to mediate the transfer of files between you and your clients.

Acrobat.com is Adobe's file sharing server. Anyone can sign up for a free Acrobat.com account and then upload files of any type to be shared. Acrobat X is well integrated with Acrobat.com to easily share files with one person, a list of people, or the entire online universe.

In This Chapter

Creating an Acrobat.com Account

The first step in using Acrobat.com is to sign up for a free account. You will need your favorite Web browser to do this.

To create an Acrobat.com account:

1. In the Web browser of your choice, go to Acrobat.com.

   When the page loads, you will be looking at a Flash-generated Welcome page .

Ⓐ Acrobat.com is Adobe's online product that offers cloud services, including free file sharing.

It Also Does This and This and *This*

This chapter discusses how to use Acrobat.com to share files with the greater population: This is the part of the service that has a direct bearing on Acrobat X use. However, Acrobat.com offers a remarkably wide range of free services.

After you log on to Acrobat.com, you have access to the following free features:

- Create a shared workspace on which you and a team of people can store files associated with a common task.

- Convert arbitrary files (images, Office files, etc.) to PDF without using Acrobat. This is just a sample of the service, because you are limited to a total of five file conversions unless you pay a fee (see below).

- Conduct live video conferences with up to two other Acrobat.com members. Coolly, you get a virtual whiteboard that everyone can see.

- Use in-the-cloud applications, including a word processor, a presentation designer, and a chart maker.

For a monthly fee, you can have a somewhat richer experience: unlimited PDF conversions, more people in your Web conference, and online customer support. The "Pro" services are pricey enough that they will be of interest mostly to corporate customers.

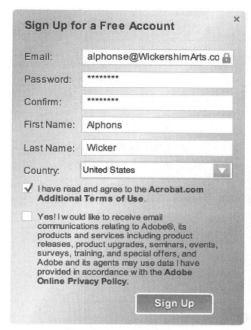

Sign Up for a Free Account ×

Email: alphonse@WickershimArts.co 🔒

Password: ********

Confirm: ********

First Name: Alphons

Last Name: Wicker

Country: United States ▼

✓ I have read and agree to the **Acrobat.com Additional Terms of Use.**

☐ Yes! I would like to receive email communications relating to Adobe®, its products and services including product releases, product upgrades, seminars, events, surveys, training, and special offers, and Adobe and its agents may use data I have provided in accordance with the **Adobe Online Privacy Policy.**

Sign Up

B To sign up for a free Acrobat.com account, just fill in the standard information and click the Sign Up button.

2. Click the Sign Up button in the upper right of the page.

You will be presented with a short form that requests the account information common to every online service you have ever joined **B**.

3. Fill in the required information and then click the Sign Up button.

Acrobat.com will work for a moment and then present you with its Organizer view **C**: The Organizer is effectively your home page where you delete, rename, and otherwise manage your shared files. This is also where you access Acrobat.com's other features (see the sidebar "It Also Does This and This and *This*").

We discuss how to manage your shared files in the Organizer later in this chapter. For now, let's explore how to share files from within Acrobat X.

TIP Acrobat.com is built on Adobe's Flash technology. Consequently, you can't access it from an iPhone or iPad.

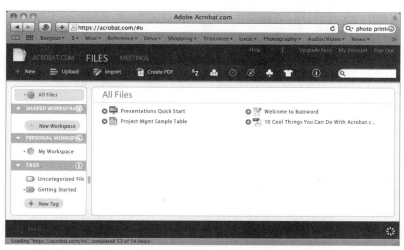

C The Organizer is your Acrobat.com home page. It shows you the files and workspaces you have on the server and provides access to the service's features.

Using the Acrobat X Share Pane

Let's return to Acrobat X for a moment.

Acrobat's Share pane lets you send a file or set of files to the Acrobat.com file server so that other people can download it to their computers 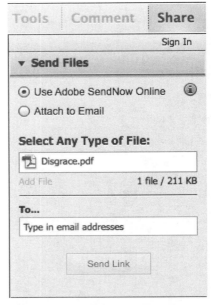; you share these files without ever leaving the Acrobat X application. If you wish, Acrobat will also send an email to one or more people, letting them know the file is available and providing a link to the shared file.

Acrobat's ability to post files to Acrobat.com is called SendNow Online.

Before you can use the Share pane to share files, you must give Acrobat X your Acrobat.com log-on information. Clicking the Sign In link at the top of the Share pane lets you log in with your email address and Acrobat.com password. A Sign Up link is available during the process in case you don't already have an Acrobat.com account.

To share a file using the Share pane:

1. Open the Share pane and sign in, if necessary.

    The Share pane is initially set up to share the current file.

2. Select the SendNow radio button, if necessary.

    This should be selected by default. See the tip for information on the other radio button, Attach to Email.

A The Share pane gives you access to the Acrobat.com file sharing features from within the Acrobat X application.

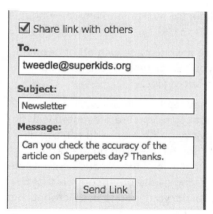

When you share a file, you supply the email addresses of the people with whom you want to share. Acrobat.com sends an email to these people, supplying them with a link to the file.

3. If you want to post additional files to Acrobat.com, click the Add Files link.

Acrobat presents you with a standard pick-a-file dialog, which you can use to select the files you want to upload.

4. If you want Acrobat to notify one or more people that the file is available, select the "Share link with others" check box. Acrobat requests the recipients' email addresses **B**.

5. Click the Send Link button.

Acrobat uploads the files to Acrobat.com and then emails a file link to the people you specified **C**.

TIP The alternative option to SendNow Online is to attach the files to an email. Click the Attach to Email radio button; an Attach button appears that, when clicked, sends you to your email client where a new email message is set up for you, complete with the attachment.

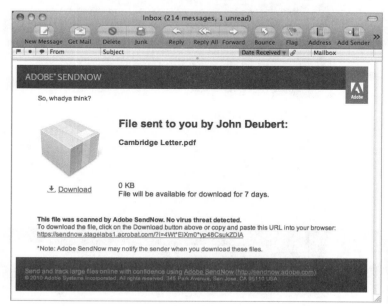

C Your recipients will receive an email message that looks like this one and contains a link to the shared file.

Using Acrobat.com

As you have seen, Acrobat lets you conveniently share files with other people on Acrobat.com. However, Acrobat.com has a broader set of services that are available if you work directly in Acrobat.com using your Web browser.

In this section, you'll learn the basics of managing the files you have uploaded to Acrobat.com. Specifically, you'll learn how to:

- Examine the files you have stored on the Acrobat.com server.
- Remove files from the server.
- Make a file available to a specific list of people.

- Make a file available to anyone who has that file's URL.
- Share a workspace with other people so you can all have access to a common set of files.

As you saw earlier, when you first sign on to Acrobat.com, you are presented with the Organizer page **Ⓐ**. Here you can see all the files you have stored on the server, buttons that invoke the various Acrobat.com features, and all the other controls that Adobe thinks you need to use Acrobat.com to its fullest.

Complete coverage of Acrobat.com's services would fill a book. Therefore, we'll discuss only those features that allow you to share files with other people.

Ⓐ The Organizer is where you start every session with Acrobat.com.

The Acrobat.com UI

Acrobat.com is based on Flash, Adobe's technology for implementing Web-based applications. As a result, Acrobat.com's interface is somewhat idiosyncratic, employing user interface features not standard to the Macintosh, Windows, or any other environment **B**.

In particular:

- Most commands are triggered by clicking links rather than a button; no visual distinction is made between links that do something and links that take you somewhere.

- Right-clicking a file in the Organizer does not yield a context menu for that file; instead, it yields a menu for Flash settings. Most of the file-related commands reside in a drop-down menu that you access by clicking a down arrow button that appears when you roll over the file.

- Some Acrobat.com commands trigger a pop-up pane in the lower-left corner of the screen. For example, when you share a file in Acrobat.com, you get a pop-up pane with links to the different kinds of sharing that are available **B**.

None of the quirkiness is particularly difficult, and you should adapt to the way Acrobat.com does things without too many moments of startlement.

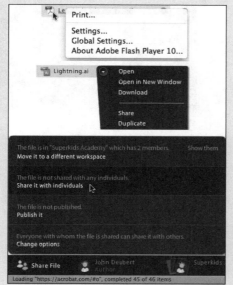

B As a consequence of Acrobat.com's Flash underpinnings, there are some unique UI features that you will quickly get used to, although they can be surprising at first.

To add or remove files on Acrobat.com:

1. Sign in to Acrobat.com with your favorite browser.

   The Organizer will appear .

2. To add a file to your Acrobat.com account, click the Upload button in the Organizer **C** and select the desired files.

   Your browser will copy the selected files to the Acrobat.com server; they will appear in the Organizer window.

3. To remove a file from Acrobat.com, move your mouse pointer over the file in the Organizer, click the down arrow that appears, and choose Delete in the drop-down menu **D**.

   Acrobat.com asks if you're sure you want to delete the file **E**; click OK.

TIP If you examine the drop-down menu in **D**, you will see a number of other commands you can use on the file, including renaming it and making a duplicate. These functions are all very easy to use.

C The Upload button is at the top of the Organizer window.

D You delete a file from Acrobat.com by choosing Delete from the file's drop-down menu.

E When you try to delete a file, you are given a chance to think better of it.

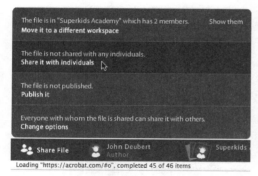

(A) To share a file with a group of specific individuals, you select the appropriate item from the pop-up pane that appears at the bottom of the Organizer window.

(B) Acrobat.com asks for the email addresses of the people with whom you want to share the file. It will send a notification to these people.

(C) The "Make them" menu lets you give various levels of file access to your readers.

TIP The curiously named "Make them" menu in the Share dialog **(C)** lets you assign access privileges to the people who access this file. You can make them one of two types of user: a Co-author who can do anything to the file except delete it or a Reader who can only look at the file contents. Be choosy about whom you let be Co-authors; they can rename, duplicate, redistribute, and otherwise manipulate the file.

Sharing Files with Acrobat.com

Acrobat.com supports three different ways to share a file with other people:

- **Share a file** with a hand-picked list of people. These people receive an emailed invitation containing a download link for the file. Only people who are on your invitation list can access the file.

- **Publish a file** so that anyone who has the link to the file can download the file.

- **Share a workspace** with a group of people. These people—presumably a team with whom you are working on a project—can access any of the files in the workspace. We'll talk about workspaces in detail in the next section of the chapter.

To share a file with a list of people:

1. In the Organizer, choose Share from the file's drop-down menu.

   Acrobat.com presents a pop-up pane of options in the lower-left corner of the window **(A)**.

2. Click the "Share it with individuals" link in the pop-up pane.

3. Type a list of comma-separated email addresses into the resulting dialog **(B)**.

   You can also type in a subject and a message.

4. Click the Share button.

   Acrobat emails a message containing a file link to your list of recipients.

To publish a file for general access:

1. In the Organizer, choose Share from the file's drop-down menu.

   Acrobat.com presents a pop-up pane of options in the lower-left corner of the window .

2. Click the "Publish it" link in the pop-up pane.

   Acrobat.com displays a dialog containing a warning that you are about to make this file available to everyone in the world, including people who don't like you much **D**.

3. Click the Publish button.

   Acrobat.com displays a little pop-up pane at the bottom of the Organizer window with links that copy the file's link to your computer's clipboard. **E**.

D When you publish a file, it will be available to anyone who knows its link. Acrobat.com gives you the chance to change your mind.

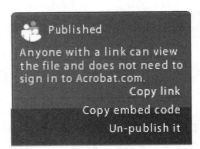

E This little pane rolls up from the bottom of the window when you publish a file. It contains copy-and-paste-able links to the file so you can email the links or embed the link on a Web page. This is also where you unpublish a file.

F You can get to the pane in **E** at any time by rolling your mouse over the Published link at the bottom of the Organizer window. This will appear only when you have selected a published file.

G The ad on this Web page resides on the Acrobat.com server. It appears here because the embed code for the file was pasted into the Web page's HTML code.

TIP After you have published a file on Acrobat.com, you can copy the link to the file at any time. Select the file in the Organizer and move your cursor over the Published link at the bottom of the window **F**; the pane pictured in **E** will immediately pop up. Click the Copy Link link in this pane. Note that the Published link appears only when you have selected a published file in the Organizer.

TIP You can also embed a published file on a Web page **G**. Just click the "Copy embed code" link in the Published pop-up pane **E**. This will copy to your clipboard the HTML code that makes the file an embedded item on a Web page **G**. Just paste this code into your Web page's HTML code. You *do* know HTML, don't you?

Working with Workspaces

Every file you upload to Acrobat.com resides in a *workspace*. Conceptually, a workspace is a place on the server where you keep a collection of related files. Workspaces let you collect in one place all of the files that apply to a particular task or project.

The left side of the Organizer lists all of the workspaces associated with your account **Ⓐ**.

When you sign in to Acrobat.com, you are looking at the contents of your *personal workspace*. Your personal workspace is where files are put when you first upload them. This workspace is available to only you; anything you place here is private.

Shared workspaces allow you to share files with a group of people, presumably members of a team working on a shared project.

Members of a shared workspace can use it just as though it were their personal space. Each member, upon signing into Acrobat.com, will find the workspace in his or her list of shared workspaces. Members can work in the shared workspace by simply clicking it in the list and then treating the workspace as though it were their own to open files, rename them, upload new files, and so on.

This is an excellent file repository for people working on a shared task.

You can move files to a shared workspace simply by dragging them from your personal workspace to the desired destination in the workspace list **Ⓑ**.

Ⓐ The Organizer lists all of your workspaces down the left side of the browser window. Shared workspaces are accessible to all members of a group; the personal workspace is yours alone.

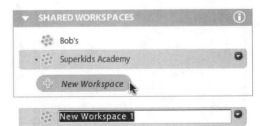

Ⓑ You place a file into a shared workspace by simply dragging it there in the Organizer.

Ⓒ You create a shared workspace by clicking the New Workspace button at the bottom of the list of shared workspaces (top). Acrobat.com creates the new workspace and lets you name it (bottom).

 Having created a shared workspace, you must tell Acrobat.com who can access it. You start by choosing Share Workspace in the workspace's drop-down menu.

 Acrobat.com asks you for the email addresses of everyone who should have access to your workspace.

TIP In the drop-down menu , you'll see there are a number of other commands you can use on your shared workspace, including deleting and renaming it. All of these functions work pretty much as you would expect.

TIP You can create folders in a workspace to organize your files, as you do on your computer. Create folders by choosing **New Folder** in the drop-down menu . Once created, they work exactly like folders on a computer.

To create a shared workspace:

1. Click the New Workspace button at the end of the list of Shared Workspaces in the Organizer .

   Acrobat.com adds a new workspace to the Shared list and highlights its initial name .

2. Type in a name for the new workspace.

3. Click the down arrow attached to the workspace's name and choose Share Workspace from the drop-down menu .

   Acrobat.com presents you with a dialog that lets you invite people to share the workspace .

4. Type in the comma-separated email addresses of the people who should have access to the workspace. You can also add a subject and message.

   Remember that Acrobat.com uses email addresses as sign-in IDs; the addresses you supply in this step will be the sign-in IDs of the people who should be allowed access to the workspace.

5. Select the "Let them administer the workspace" check box if you want group members to be able to invite other people into the workspace, rename the workspace, and otherwise change the characteristics of the workspace.

6. Click the Share button.

   Acrobat.com will send these people an email to let them know they're among the chosen few who can access this workspace.

Applying Tags to Files

After a while your Acrobat.com workspace will become crowded with files from a dozen different projects that compete for your eyeballs when you stare at the Organizer.

Acrobat.com allows you to apply a text tag to files and then, through a process called *filtering*, display only files with a particular tag. Then you'll see only the files that interest you at that time.

The Organizer lists the tags known within your Acrobat.com workspace at the left side of the window, just below the list of workspaces **A**. If you click one of these tags, the Organizer will display only files with that tag. Only one of these tags can be active at a time.

To apply a tag to a file:

1. In the file's drop-down menu, choose Tag.

   Acrobat.com presents you with a list of all the currently existing tags **B**.

2. Either click one or more of the known tags or click the New Tag button and type in a new tag **C**.

3. Click OK.

   Acrobat applies the tag to the file. If you typed in a new tag, it will be added to the Organizer's list.

> **TIP** In the Organizer, you can select more than one file in the usual fashion: Shift-click selects a contiguous range of files; Ctrl-click (Command-click) selects a discontiguous set.

> **TIP** You can create a new tag without applying it to a file by clicking the New Tag button at the bottom of the Organizer's list of tags **A**.

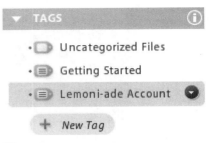

A The Organizer displays a list of all the tags known within the current workspace. There's also a New Tag button, which creates a new tag without applying it to a file.

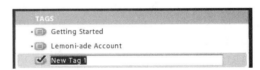

B When you apply a tag to a file, you can pick from a list of existing tags or click the New Tag button and create a new tag.

C The New Tag button adds a new, generically named tag to the list; simply type in the text you want for that tag.

6

PDF Portfolios

PDF portfolios were introduced in Acrobat 9 as a way of bundling a collection of individual files of any type into a single, PDF-compatible package. Portfolios have been refined in Acrobat X; they have new features and are easier to create.

Files within a portfolio can be any of a wide variety of types, including Microsoft Word documents, Microsoft Excel spreadsheets, Microsoft PowerPoint presentations, Apple QuickTime movies, JPEG images, Adobe Flash animations, and PDF documents. Each file within the portfolio retains its own identity; security settings and other characteristics of the document remain unchanged.

The purpose of the portfolios is to let you assemble a set of related documents for easy emailing, posting, or otherwise distributing. Thus, a portfolio might contain all the files associated with an invoice: the cover letter, the invoice itself, the summary of expenses, the scanned receipts.

Examining a Portfolio

When you open a PDF portfolio in Acrobat 9 or later, you see a display of its individual component files **A**.

To see portfolio components:

1. Double-click a file in the window to display a preview of that component file within the portfolio **B**.

A The initial view of an Acrobat X portfolio offers a representation of the files it contains.

B When you double-click a portfolio member, Acrobat displays a preview of that file.

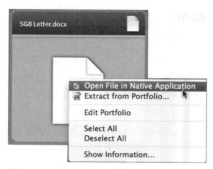

C Right-clicking (Control-clicking) a portfolio member lets you open the file in its original application or extract the original file, saving it to disk.

D A portfolio may contain folders that contain additional files or folders.

E When you open a portfolio in Acrobat 8 or earlier, you get a basic list that displays the members' contents.

2. Right-click (Control-click) the portfolio component to open the file in its original application or extract it, saving it as a separate file **C**.

TIP Portfolios have a hierarchical structure; your portfolio may contain folders **D**. Just double-click a folder to display its contents.

TIP If you open a portfolio file with an earlier version of Acrobat, you will see a window with two panes **E**. The upper pane displays the portfolio contents as a simple list; clicking an item in the list displays the contents of that item in the lower pane. This is not nearly as useful or slick as opening the file in Acrobat X or Adobe Reader X, but you can at least see the portfolio's contents.

Creating a Portfolio

Creating a portfolio requires several steps:

1. Create the portfolio with an initial layout.
2. Add files to the portfolio.
3. Select a theme for the layout.
4. Pick a color palette (optional).
5. Save the portfolio.

The portfolio user interface encourages you to do these steps in this order, but all the steps after the first step can be done in any order.

To create a portfolio:

1. Choose File > Create > PDF Portfolio.

   Acrobat presents you with the Create PDF Portfolio dialog **A**.

2. Select a layout from the list on the left side of the dialog.

   We'll discuss these layouts in detail later in the chapter; for now, the small preview on the right side of the dialog gives you an idea of what the layouts look like.

   You can change this layout later.

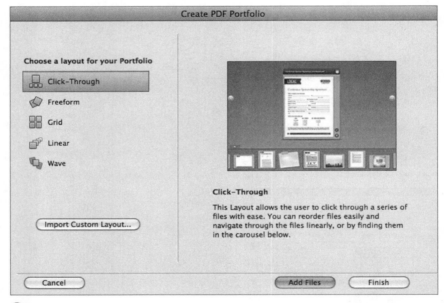

A The first step in creating a portfolio is to pick a layout.

3. If you want to add files, click Add Files and select a set of component files in the resulting pick-a-file dialog; if you don't wish to add files, click Finish.

Either way, Acrobat creates a new portfolio and displays the Portfolio Editor window **B**.

This window is modeled on the standard PDF document window, with a single toolbar running along the top and an area shared by three panes along the right side. Most of the useful tools in this window reside in the Layout pane, pictured in the figure.

continues on next page

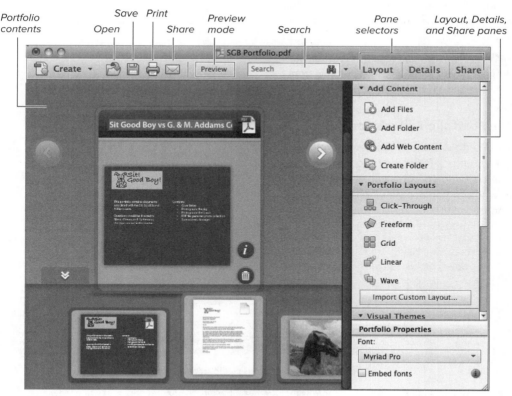

B The Portfolio Editor window has all the tools you need to specify a portfolio's components, appearance, and behavior.

4. Add files to the portfolio using the tools in the Layout pane's Add Content panel **C**.

   We'll talk about the choices here in more detail later.

5. Select File > Save Portfolio.

   Acrobat presents you with a standard save-a-file dialog, letting you save your new portfolio on your hard disk.

   Note that there's also a Save tool in the portfolio window's toolbar.

The preceding steps leave you looking at the Portfolio Editor. You can continue tweaking the portfolio until you are happy: add more files, pick a color palette, or change the layout. Much of the rest of this chapter describes how to use the controls in this editor.

TIP You can also add files to a portfolio by dragging them to the portfolio window from the Finder or Windows Explorer.

C The Add Content panel in the Layout pane has the tools you need to add files, folders, and Web content to your portfolio.

The Portfolio Editor's toolbar

The Portfolio Editor's toolbar provides a set of buttons for common commands **D**. The collection of tools will vary according to whether you are viewing or editing the portfolio, although most tools are common to both modes.

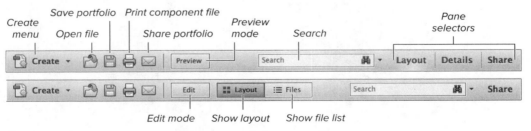

D The Portfolio Editor's toolbar has controls that are available when creating (top) and when viewing (bottom) a portfolio.

- **Create.** This is a drop-down menu identical to the File > Create submenu.

- **Open.** This tool lets you select a file to open in Acrobat; it is identical to the menu item File > Open.

- **Save.** This tool saves the portfolio to disk; it is identical to the menu item File > Save Portfolio.

- **Print.** This tool prints the current component file. Unfortunately, it works only with PDF components.

- **Share.** This tool lets you share the portfolio as an email attachment or by using Adobe SendNow. See Chapter 5 for details on how file sharing works in Acrobat X.

- **Preview / Edit.** These two buttons let you switch between Preview mode (used for viewing the portfolio) and Edit mode (in which you modify the portfolio). Predictably, the Preview button is visible only in Edit mode and vice versa.

- **Layout / Files (Preview mode only).** These two buttons let you decide how the files should be displayed in Preview mode. The Layout button displays the portfolio using its specified layout (Linear, Click-Through, etc.). The Files button presents the component files as a compact list **E**: This is an efficient, compact, if not very pretty, display of the files in the portfolio.

- **Search.** This is a standard search field that lets you search for text within the portfolio's component documents.

continues on next page

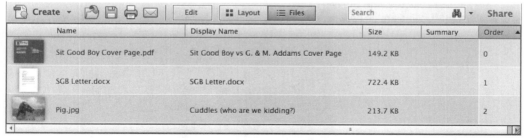

E The list view is a very compact representation of all the member files of a portfolio.

- **Layout (Edit mode only).** This is a trigger that makes the Layout pane visible. The Layout pane contains tools that let you modify the appearance of your portfolio ⒡: It is what you use to select a theme or a color palette, for example.

- **Details (Edit mode only).** This makes the Details pane visible ⒢. This pane contains a series of check boxes that let you specify what information should be displayed for each file in List mode ⒠.

- **Share.** This is the standard Share pane, as discussed in Chapter 5.

TIP The list view ⒠ is especially useful when working with very large portfolios; the usual layout animation and presentation becomes less useful with a large number of component files.

TIP The only change I've ever been tempted to make in the Details pane ⒢ is to select the Created check mark. Otherwise, the useful items are already selected, and the can't-see-why-you'd-want-it items are all deselected.

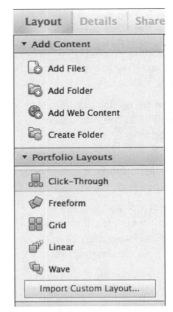

⒡ The Layout pane has all the tools you use to modify a portfolio.

⒢ The Details pane lets you specify what information should be presented to the user when viewing the portfolio's file list ⒠.

A The Create Portfolio dialog has an Add Files button that lets you import an initial set of files into the portfolio at the time you create it.

B The Add Content panel is the best place to add files and other content to your portfolio.

Adding Files

There are several ways to add files to a portfolio:

- You can add an initial collection of files when you first create the portfolio by clicking the Add Files button in the Create Portfolio dialog **A**.

- You can drag files and folders from the Finder or Windows Explorer to the portfolio window.

- You can use the tools in the Add Content panel of the Layout pane **B**.

The Add Content panel gives you the most capability; its four tools include:

- **Add Files.** No surprises here: Acrobat presents you with a pick-a-file dialog and lets you select one or more files to add to the portfolio.

- **Add Folder.** This lets you choose a folder on your hard disk; Acrobat adds the folder and all of its contents to the portfolio. If the folder contains other folders, those (and their contents) will be added also.

- **Add Web Content.** This is a new bit of Acrobat X coolness: You can add a Web page to your portfolio. Acrobat will ask you for the URL and then create a small Web document, which is added to the portfolio. Your layout will show a preview of the Web page. See the following section, "Adding Web Content," for more information.

continues on next page

- **Create Folder.** This creates a new folder inside your portfolio. Once created, you can treat it like a folder on your computer: drag items into it from your computer desktop or elsewhere in the portfolio, and examine its contents by double-clicking on it . This folder exists only within the portfolio; it doesn't reside anywhere on your disk.

TIP Be careful when adding folders from your disk to a portfolio; large folders can take a *very* long time to add. An excellent way to bring Acrobat to its knees is to drag your hard disk icon into the portfolio window; you can sit and watch the spinning beach ball or rotating hourglass for several hours while Acrobat tries to cram the entire contents of your hard disk into the portfolio.

TIP On Mac OS X, many items that look like files are actually folders (called *packages*) that are treated specially by the operating system. Executable application files are the most common examples of this, but it may be true of document files, as well. Unfortunately, Acrobat X doesn't seem to know what to make of these files; it refuses to add them to a portfolio unless you drag them from the Finder/ Windows Explorer, in which case they are stored in the portfolio as a folder.

C Folders within a portfolio behave just like their desktop equivalents. Add files to them by dragging; double-click to see their contents.

Adding Web content

When you click the Add Web Content tool in the Layout pane, Acrobat presents you with the Add Web Content dialog **D**. This dialog collects the following information from you:

- **File Name.** This is the name of the small Web file that Acrobat will create within the portfolio when it imports the Web content. This file exists only within the portfolio; it does not live directly on your disk.

- **Description.** This is a phrase that describes the content.

- **Add a Web Link / Embed Tag.** These radio buttons let you specify the nature of the Web content you are importing. A Web link is a standard URL, linking to a page on the Web. An embed tag is a snippet of HTML, often copied from YouTube or a similar Web site, that points to a picture or movie embedded on a Web page.

- **URL / Embed Tag text.** Finally, you need to supply the URL of the Web page or the embed code of the item you want to place in the portfolio.

TIP What gets stored in your portfolio is a link to the Web page or embedded item, not the actual page or item. Thus, adding Web content has only a tiny effect on your portfolio's size.

TIP Interestingly, Acrobat also lets you go in the other direction: You can export your portfolio as a Web site (choose File > Save PDF Portfolio as Web Site). This isn't for novices, but if you're comfortable uploading files to your Web server using FTP software, you may want to explore this feature.

Layouts and Themes

In an effort to simplify the creation of sophisticated-looking portfolios, Adobe introduced the notions of layouts and themes to Acrobat X. Layouts actually existed in Acrobat 9, but they have acquired a new prominence in this new version of the software.

A *layout* determines how a portfolio's component files are arranged in the portfolio window and how you choose among those files. A *theme* specifies the appearance of the layout's components: the background image that should be used, the color palette, the kind of frame around the file previews, and so on. Each layout has a default theme, but this can be changed in the Layout pane, as you will see.

Layouts and themes are predefined items; you select them from lists. Although you are compelled to choose a layout when you initially create a portfolio, you can change this layout and pick a different theme from the Layout pane **A**.

Acrobat X ships with five layouts:

- **Click-Through.** This presents a single component file at a time, with a "film-strip" running along the bottom that lets you move among the files as desired. This layout is for cases where the components have an order to them, but it is okay for the reader to jump around **B**.

A The Layout pane lets you select a layout and theme for your portfolio.

B The Click-Through layout specifies a sequence for the portfolio contents but still allows the reader to jump around among the files.

C The Linear layout requires the reader to move through the component files in order.

D The Freeform layout scatters the component files on a background, rather like cards on a table.

- **Linear.** This presents a single file at a time, but there is no mechanism for jumping around among the files; you must view them in order **C**.

- **Freeform.** In this layout the components are scattered around the window, rather like playing cards on a table **D**. The components don't have an order and are presented in a somewhat playful manner. (Do *not* use this for year-end financial statements; trust me, your accounting department doesn't take well to "playful.")

continues on next page

- **Grid.** This is a straightforward presentation of the components in a rectangular layout **E**. It invites readers to examine the documents in their own order.

- **Wave.** This is an artsy version of Click-Through. It shows one document at a time with a filmstrip at the bottom; other components are visible as a blurry background **F**. When you move from one component to another, the visible files rearrange themselves with a fancy, impossible-to-describe animation. Use this to give your Click-Through portfolios a little pizzazz. (But note that your accounting department doesn't like artsy or pizzazz, either; know your audience.)

In all five layouts, double-clicking a component file displays the contents of that file.

Each layout has navigation controls appropriate to that layout. For example, Linear and Click-Through have arrowheads pointing right and left, allowing you to slide the file selection in those directions. Most of these controls are reasonably intuitive, so you should experiment with them.

As mentioned earlier, a **visual theme** dictates the appearance of a portfolio's layout.

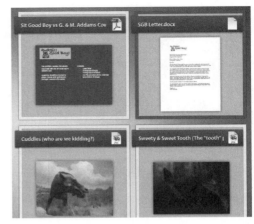

E The Grid layout displays the component files in a rectangular grid.

F The Wave layout is functionally the same as Click-Through: The files have a definite order, but you can still skip around among them. It's prettier, though.

G A visual theme changes the appearance of the portfolio's background, frame, controls, and other visual elements.

That is, the layout controls how the files are arranged in the window and how you move among them, whereas the theme specifies the color palette, background, and appearance of the buttons, frames, and other visual elements **G**.

Just as with layouts, you set your portfolio's theme by selecting it from a predefined list in the Layout pane **A**. Acrobat X ships with an initial list of five themes:

- Clean
- Spring
- Tech Office
- Modern
- Translucent

You will need to try these to see what they look like.

To change a portfolio's layout and theme:

1. Click the Edit button in the Portfolio Editor's toolbar, if necessary, to enter Edit mode.

2. Open the Layout pane, if necessary **A**.

3. Open the Portfolio Layouts panel (part of the Layout pane) and choose the layout you want to use for your portfolio.

4. Open the Visual Themes panel and click the theme you want to use for your portfolio.

TIP Acrobat X makes it possible for software developers to create new layouts and themes. You can add these custom elements to the list by clicking the Import Custom Layout or Import Custom Theme buttons at the bottom of their respective panels.

Choosing a Color Palette

By default, a portfolio's background, window frames, and so on are rendered in a set of colors dictated by the layout's visual theme. You can change this by specifying a color palette for your portfolio.

The color palette affects the color of everything in the portfolio window except the colors of the actual component documents. You can select from among a collection of predefined color palettes or create your own from scratch.

To choose a color palette:

1. In the Layout pane, open the Color Palettes panel **A**.
2. Do either of the following:
   - Click one of the rows of colored squares to select a predefined color palette.
   - Click the Create from Existing button and then choose whatever colors you want from the resulting color picker **B**.

   Note that you need to choose a color for each of the five parts that make up a portfolio page.

TIP The color picker **B** lets you specify each color either by using the visual color picker at the top of the panel or by typing a color value into a text box. For the record, the color value consists of a six-character hexadecimal RGB value. Personally, I'd rather stick with the color picker controls.

TIP Many companies have standard, corporate colors that you should use if you are creating a portfolio for use as marketing or other official materials.

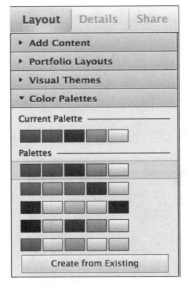

A The Color Palettes panel lets you choose from a set of predefined sets of colors that your visual theme should use.

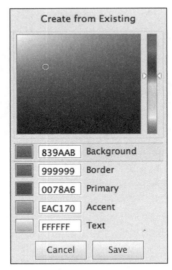

B You can also create a custom color scheme, specifying the colors of all the components of a portfolio page.

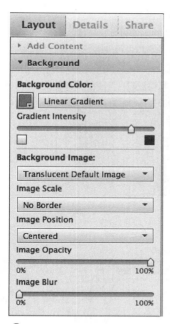

A The Background panel lets you specify a background color and image for your portfolio.

B In a linear gradient (left), brightness varies from top to bottom; in a radial gradient (right), brightness changes from the center, outward.

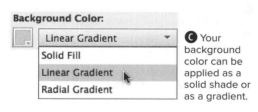

C Your background color can be applied as a solid shade or as a gradient.

Setting a Background

The visual theme you pick has an image that it uses as the background to the files it displays. For example, the Tech Office theme uses a picture of a wooden desktop; Clean has a gray, textured surface.

You can change this background to a color, an image of your own choosing, or both. You do this with the controls in the Background panel of the Layout pane A.

The Background panel lets you specify a background color and an image. The image overlays the color, blocking it from view. However, you can apply an opacity to the image that allows some of the background color to show through; the lower the image's opacity, the more the background color will be visible.

The background color can have a gradient applied to it, in which the brightness varies smoothly across the screen B. You have a choice of a linear gradient, varying from dark to light vertically in the window, or a radial gradient, whose brightness changes as you move outward from the center of the screen.

To set the background for a portfolio:

1. In the Layout pane, open the Background panel A.

2. In the Background Color drop-down menu, choose Solid Fill or one of the gradient types C.

continues on next page

3. Click the Background Color color well control and select a color **D**.

4. In the Background Image drop-down menu, select Choose New **E**.

   Acrobat presents you with a pick-a-file dialog.

5. Choose the image file you want to use as a background.

   The image will appear as your portfolio's background.

6. Adjust the Image Opacity so the background color and gradient show through to the extent you desire **F**.

7. Adjust the Image Blur slider to taste.

   You may want the background image blurred out to keep it from visually distracting the reader from the document previews **G**.

Also available are drop-down menus that let you specify the scale and position of your image, but they're easy to use and understand, so you can explore them on your own.

TIP Surprisingly, the only image types you can use as a background are JPEG and PNG. You cannot use TIFF, EPS, or (this is especially surprising) PDF graphics.

TIP In step 5, you can also select the current theme's default image or None.

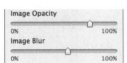

F The Opacity slider controls how much the background color shows through your image. The Blur control lets you unfocus your image so it's less distracting.

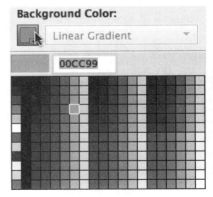

D Clicking the color well lets you specify the color you want for your background.

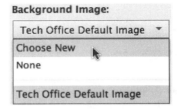

E The Background Image menu lets you choose a new image for your background. You can also have no image in the background or pick the current theme's default.

G It's usually best to have a blurry background image; otherwise, it will tend to distract the reader from the portfolio contents.

Adding Comments to a Document

One of the longest-standing features in Acrobat is the ability to add comments to a PDF document. Originally, these comments were simple, electronic sticky notes that a reader could attach to the page. The PDF annotation mechanism has since grown to include a broad set of highlighting, drawing, and other tools that you can use to do full-featured commentary on a document. Additionally, there are tools for reading and summarizing these comments, and even for conducting a document review involving your entire workgroup or company.

The annotation feature in Acrobat is so extensive and important that it occupies the next three chapters in this book, concentrating on adding comments to a PDF document, reading and managing those documents, and conducting a shared review of a document.

In This Chapter

Examining Acrobat's Comment Tools

Acrobat's comment tools reside in the Comment pane, one of the Tasks panes that live on the right side of a document window **A**.

The tools in this pane are divided into two categories:

- **Annotations** are comments that appear on the page as predefined icons. These include sticky notes, virtual rubber stamps, and a nice collection of text annotation tools.

- **Drawing Markups** are comments whose purpose is to draw something on the page, usually to draw attention to a particular element of the page. These include circles, arrows, and cute little cloud balloons.

By default, the Sticky Note and Highlight Text tools are available on the Quick Tools toolbar. However, you can add any or all of the commenting tools to the toolbar, as described in Chapter 1 **B**.

Comment icons and pop-ups

Every comment on a page has two visual parts. A comment's *icon* is a graphic that indicates the position of the comment on the page **C**. The icon differs for each comment type: a speech bubble for a sticky note, a piece of text for a text box, and a Sign Here pointer (or other graphic) for a stamp.

Most comments also have a pop-up window that displays the text associated with the comment **D**. Double-clicking the comment's icon opens its pop-up, allowing you to read and edit the comment's text.

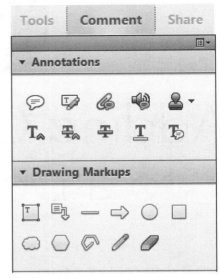

A The Acrobat X commenting tools display in two panels in the Comment pane.

B Any of the commenting tools can be added to the Quick Tools toolbar.

C Every comment has an icon that indicates its position on the page.

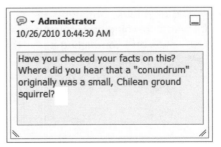

D Most comments have a pop-up window that holds the text for that comment.

TIP Acrobat's Preferences dialog has a pane full of controls determining the behavior of comments **E**. The default values for these options are sensible, so you can safely ignore them. However, once you've worked with comments for a while, you may want to take a look at them. Choose Edit > Preferences, or Acrobat > Preferences on a Mac, to access Acrobat's Preferences.

TIP The first time you use some of Acrobat's comment tools, you may be presented with a dialog that asks for your name, company, and so on **F**. If you choose to provide this information, Acrobat uses it for some of the dynamic comments that add your name and other data to the comment on the fly.

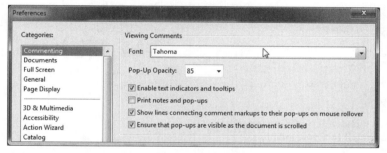

E The Acrobat X Preferences include a set of controls that affect the appearance and behavior of comments.

F When you first use the comment tools, Acrobat may ask you for some identification information. This is strictly optional.

Adding a Sticky Note Comment

The sticky note comment is Acrobat's oldest annotation type, dating back to Acrobat 1.0. This annotation type is the functional equivalent of the paper sticky note after which it's named; it holds a small amount of text attached to the page in a pop-up window.

To add a sticky note to a page:

1. Click the Sticky Note tool in the Annotations panel of the Comment pane.

The pointer turns into crosshairs.

2. Click the page.

Acrobat places the comment's icon on the page and opens the comment's pop-up window.

3. Type your comment text into the pop-up window **A**.

TIP To change the location of a comment's icon, click and drag it to a new location.

TIP You can change the text of an existing comment. To do so, double-click the icon to get to the pop-up window and then click the text and edit it as usual. This works with any type of comment that has text (which is most types of comment).

A sticky note's default icon is a speech bubble. This is a perfectly serviceable icon, but Acrobat supplies a collection of other icons that may be used for sticky note comments **B**.

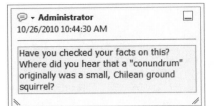

A When you place a sticky note on the page, Acrobat opens a pop-up window into which you can type your text.

B Sticky notes can be represented on the page by an assortment of icons.

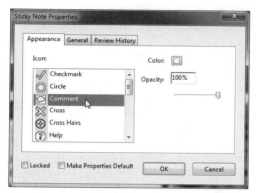

C You change a sticky note's icon (and other characteristics) by modifying its properties.

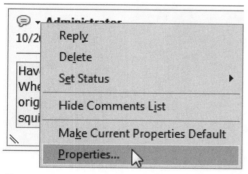

D The Sticky Note Properties dialog lets you modify a variety of Appearance settings.

E You can also access a comment's properties by clicking the tiny down arrow in its pop-up window.

To change a sticky note's icon:

1. Right-click (Control-click) the sticky note comment's icon to get a context menu.

2. Choose Properties in the context menu **C**.

    Acrobat presents you with the Sticky Note Properties dialog **D**.

3. Choose a new icon from the list.

4. If you want this icon to become the default icon for future sticky note comments, select the Make Properties Default check box.

5. To change the note's color, click the square Color control and choose a new color from the resulting color picker.

6. To change the opacity of the note, drag the Opacity slider to the desired level or type a number in the Opacity percentage field.

7. Click OK.

TIP You can prevent a comment from being edited by selecting the Locked check box in the Sticky Note Properties dialog **D**. This check box appears in the Properties dialog of all the annotation types.

TIP You can delete a comment the way you delete most everything else in the computer world: Select it, and then press the Delete key.

TIP You can also access a comment's context menu by clicking the tiny down arrow in the upper-left corner of its pop-up window **E**.

Adding a Text Box Comment

A text box comment is similar to a sticky note, but it has no pop-up window. Instead, the comment displays its text in a rectangular, editable field directly on the page **A**.

To place a text box on the page:

1. Click the Text Box tool [T] in the Drawing Markups panel.

2. Click and drag a rectangle on the page. Acrobat places the text box at that location on the page.

3. Type your comment into the text box.

Having placed your text box on the page, you can move it and resize it very easily.

To move and resize a text box:

1. Click the text box.

   Handles appear at the sides and corners of the text box **B**.

2. Click and drag the text box to change its position on the page.

   Note that the text will rearrange its line breaks, if necessary, to accommodate the new size of the box.

3. Click and drag one of the handles to change the box's size.

You can also control a text box's appearance to quite a large extent. Following are instructions for changing some of these characteristics.

This page should be removed. If possible, it should also be burned.

A A text box comment presents a text annotation in a rectangular field placed directly on the page.

This page should be removed. If possible, it should also be burned.

B When you select a text box's text, handles appear at the corners and sides.

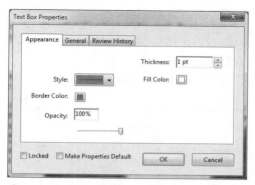

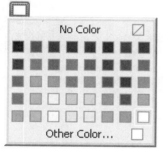

C The Text Box Properties dialog lets you change the appearance of the box that contains the text.

Fill Color:

D Clicking one of the color well controls results in a standard color picker.

To change a text box's colors:

1. Right-click (Control-click) the text box to access a context menu.

2. Select Properties at the bottom of the context menu.

   Acrobat presents you with the Text Box Properties dialog **C**.

3. Click the square Border Color control. The color well drops down a standard color picker **D**.

4. Choose the color you want for your border.

5. To choose a fill color, repeat steps 3 and 4, clicking the square Fill Color control **C**.

6. Click OK.

Finally, you can change the font and other characteristics of the text inside the text box. This takes a bit more effort, because you need to use the well-hidden Properties toolbar **E**.

TIP In the Text Box Properties dialog, you can also change the style and thickness of the text box's border as well as the box's opacity. Feel free to experiment with these settings.

E The Text Box Text Properties toolbar presents information on whatever is selected on the page. You can use it to change the characteristics of text.

To change a text box's font and text size:

1. Make the Properties toolbar visible, if necessary; to do so, right-click (Control-click) the Quick Tools or Favorites toolbar and select Properties Bar from the context menu.

2. Double-click the text in the text box.

   A blinking cursor appears at the point where you double-clicked.

3. Choose the text in the text box whose font or size you want to change.

   The Properties toolbar reports the current font and size.

4. In the Properties toolbar, change the font and size to the values you want.

5. Click outside the text box to finish.

TIP The Properties toolbar lets you change many characteristics of your text box text, including alignment, color, and placement above or below the baseline **F**.

TIP You can also change the style of your text to some combination of bold and italic. After selecting text in the text box (step 3 in the preceding task), right-click (Control-click) the text, and choose Text Style **G**.

TIP The Properties toolbar lets you change a variety of properties for all the annotation types, although the precise properties you can change depends on what type of comment it is. For example, in a sticky note, you can change the style of the text and the color of the background but not the font or size.

I *think* that I shall never see
A buzzer **louder** than a bee
A bee whose pointy little rear
Makes **me** run away in fear

F Using the Properties toolbar, you can change the font, size, and style of your text box text.

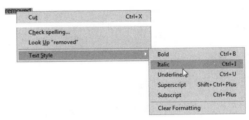

G You can also change the style of your text box text via the Text Style submenu.

I don't understand this illustration.

A A callout comment is just a text box with an arrow.

I don't understand this illustration.

B Clicking a callout gives you handles you can use to position the box and its arrow.

Adding a Callout Comment

A callout comment is a text box with an arrow attached **A**. It lets you point to the object on the page that has raised the comment.

To add a callout to a page:

1. In the Drawing Markups panel, select the Callout tool.

2. Click and drag a rectangle on the page.

   Acrobat adds a callout comment with a default arrow pointing at nothing in particular.

3. Type your comment into the text field.

4. Click the border of the comment to make handles appear **B**.

5. Drag the handles to position the arrow and text box as you want it.

A callout comment has the same set of properties as a text box comment (font, point size, and so on). See the previous section for a discussion of these properties and instructions on how to change them.

Adding Lines and Arrows

Several of Acrobat's commenting tools let you add graphic items to your document's pages. The Line and Arrow tools let you add lines and arrows to the page 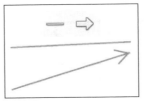.

To add a line or an arrow to the page:

1. Click the Line or Arrow tool in the Drawing Markups panel.

2. Click and hold on the page at one end of your line or arrow.

3. Drag to where you want the other end of the line or arrow to go.

4. Release the mouse button.

> **TIP** Lines can be turned into arrows and vice versa. In the Properties dialog (right-click [Control-click] the item and select Properties), you can apply an End type to the line . A value of None turns an arrow into a line; a value of Open (for open arrow) turns a line into an arrow. You can choose from several other line ends.

> **TIP** You can reverse an arrow by right-clicking (Control-clicking) it and selecting Flip Line.

> **TIP** Lines and arrows can have text comments associated with them. Double-click the line or arrow to see its pop-up window. Even when the pop-up window is closed, you can tell that an arrow or a line (or any graphic annotation) has a text comment because Acrobat adds a tiny speech bubble to it **C**.

A The Arrow and Line tools let you draw arrows and lines on the page. This explains their names.

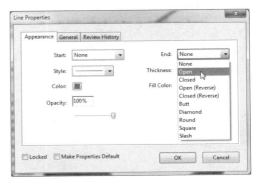

B The Line Properties dialog lets you add an End to a line, converting it into an arrow, for example. Choosing None turns an arrow into a line.

C A comment icon that has text associated with it displays a tiny speech bubble.

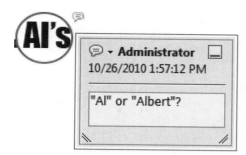

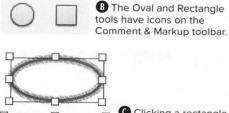

A You can use the Oval tool to draw attention to items of interest on the page.

B The Oval and Rectangle tools have icons on the Comment & Markup toolbar.

C Clicking a rectangle or an oval icon produces handles you can use to resize that icon.

Drawing Ovals and Rectangles

The Oval and Rectangle comment tools let you call attention to items on the Acrobat page **A**.

To add an oval or rectangle comment to the page:

1. Click the Oval or Rectangle tool in the Drawing Markups panel **B**.

   The pointer changes to crosshairs.

2. Click and drag the crosshairs on the page. Acrobat draws a rectangle or an oval as you drag.

3. Release the mouse button.

   Acrobat adds the oval or rectangle to the page.

4. Click the oval or rectangle.

   Acrobat adds handles to the sides and corners **C**.

5. Reposition and resize the oval or rectangle as you desire.

TIP You can create a perfect square or circle by holding down the Alt (Option) key while clicking and dragging in step 2.

Adding Polygons and Clouds

The polygon-related comment tools work the way similar tools work in most graphics software: You click sequentially on the vertices of the shape you want, and Acrobat connects the dots, making the polygon. Acrobat supplies three polygon annotation tools in the Drawing Markups panel :

- **Polygon tool.** This tool creates a closed polygon. When you're finished clicking vertices, Acrobat adds a final side that connects the last point with the first.

- **Polygon Line tool.** This is identical to the Polygon tool except that Acrobat doesn't close the figure for you.

- **Cloud tool.** This is identical to the Polygon tool except that Acrobat draws the polygon as a cloud **A**. Your legal and accounting departments will think these frivolous.

A The three polygon-related comment tools are Cloud, Polygon, and Polygon Line.

To add a polygon or cloud to a page:

1. Select the Cloud, Polygon, or Polygon Line tool in the Drawing Markups panel.

2. Click the starting point of your polygon or cloud.

3. Click sequentially on all the corners in your polygon or cloud.

   Acrobat draws the line segments as you go so you can see how your polygon or cloud looks.

4. Double-click the final point to finish the polygon or cloud.

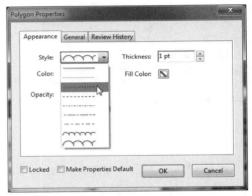

B You can turn a polygon into a cloud by changing its line style.

TIP You can convert polygons to clouds and vice versa. Right-click (Control-click) the comment, and look at its properties. One of the controls is a pop-up menu of line styles **B**. Choose one of the cloud styles to convert your polygon to a cloud.

A The text markup tools reside in the Annotations panel in the Comment pane.

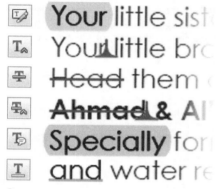

B Acrobat provides all the tools you need to do full text markup on an Acrobat file.

Text Edits

Acrobat provides a complete set of tools for indicating changes that need to be made to text on a page. These include annotations to mark text for replacement and deletion, and to mark an insertion point for missing text.

The tools you use to do this reside in the Annotations panel of the Comment pane **A**.

The markup tools in Acrobat are as follows, from top to bottom in **B**:

- **Highlight Selected Text** adds a colored backdrop to the selected text to draw attention to it.

- **Insert Text at Cursor** indicates that text should be inserted into the existing words. A little caret appears at the place you click in the text. The pop-up window associated with the annotation contains the new text.

- **Crossout Text for Deletion** strikes through the selected text, indicating that it should be removed.

- **Replace Selected Text** strikes through the selected text, indicating that it should be removed, and places an insert-text caret at the end, indicating that new text should be inserted. The pop-up window associated with the annotation contains the new text.

continues on next page

- **Add Note to Selected Text** highlights the text. The pop-up window associated with the annotation contains a comment about the text. This seems to be in every way identical to the Highlight Text tool except that Acrobat automatically opens the pop-up window so you can type your comment.
- **Underline Selected Text** underlines the text for emphasis.

All of these tools are very easy to use.

To add text markup to a page:

1. In the Annotations panel, click the tool you want to use.

   The pointer turns into an I-beam shape.

2. Select the text to which you want to apply the markup annotation.

   Acrobat immediately applies the markup. If your markup requires insertion or notation text, a pop-up window opens so you can type your text.

   TIP You can change the color of the text markup (the highlight or underline stroke). Just right-click (Control-click) the markup and select Properties. The resulting dialog provides a standard color control (as well as some other useful buttons) **C**.

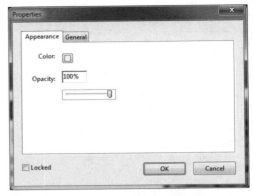

C The text markup Properties dialog lets you change the color and opacity of a text markup.

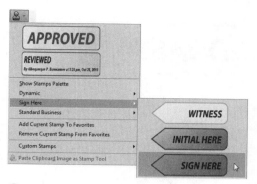

A Like a rubber stamp, the Stamp tool lets you place predefined graphics on the page.

Adding a Stamp Comment

One of the most popular annotation types (well, *I* like it) is the stamp. This comment type is modeled on the traditional rubber stamp once popular with banks and still popular with four-year-old children.

The Stamp tool, in the Annotations panel, actually is a drop-down menu that gives you access to all the stamp annotations **A**.

The stamps are organized into categories: Dynamic, Sign Here, and Standard Business are provided by default. You can also compile your own Favorites menu, containing stamps you particularly like.

At the top of the Stamp submenu may be a series of Favorites (the Approved and Reviewed stamps in **A**). These provide quick access to your frequently used stamps. You'll learn how to add stamps to this menu shortly.

Note that some of the stamps are dynamic, incorporating the identity data you may have supplied when you first started using the comment tools. (We talked about this at the start of the chapter.)

You can create your own stamps and your own categories. The Acrobat version of a stamp lets you use any PDF graphic—any combination of text, line art, and images—as your rubber stamp. You'll learn how to do this in the next section.

To apply a stamp to the page:

1. In the Stamp menu , choose the category and stamp you want.

   The pointer turns into a ghostly version of the stamp you choose.

2. Click on the page where you want your stamp to go.

   Acrobat places the stamp on the page in its default size.

3. Click the stamp image on the page to select it.

   Handles appear at the corners of the stamp **B**.

4. Click and drag the handles to make the stamp the size you want. You can also rotate the stamp by dragging the handle-on-a-stick rising above it **C**.

TIP While a stamp is selected, you can add the stamp to your favorites by selecting Add Current Stamp To Favorites in the Stamp menu **A**.

Creating your own stamp

It is remarkably easy to create your own stamp comment for use with the Stamp tool. You can take graphics, text, or images from any PDF file and turn them into a stamp. You can even create new categories for your stamps.

To create a stamp:

1. From the Stamp tool's menu, choose Create Custom Stamp **D**.

   Acrobat presents you with the Select Image for Custom Stamp dialog **E**.

B Clicking a stamp yields handles you can use to resize and rotate it.

C You rotate a stamp by dragging the handle-on-a-stick.

D To create your own stamp, choose Create Custom Stamp from the Stamp menu.

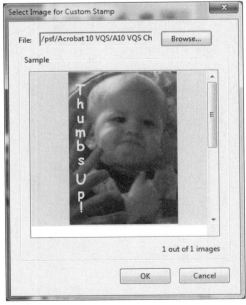

E Select a file as the source for your stamp's graphic.

F Give your new stamp a name and assign it to a category. You can also type a new category name.

G Your new category and stamp appear in the Stamp menu.

H You can paste clipboard contents onto the page as a stamp.

2. Click the Browse button.

The standard Open dialog opens.

3. Choose the file that contains the art-work you want to use for your stamp.

This can be a PDF file or any type of file that Acrobat can convert to PDF. Acrobat displays the first page of the document in the dialog.

4. Using the scroll bar, select the page in the document that you want to use as your stamp.

5. Click OK.

The Create Custom Stamp dialog opens F.

6. Choose a category to which to add your stamp, or if you like, type the name of a new category.

7. Type a name for your new stamp.

8. Click OK.

Your new stamp (and new category, if you made one) appears among the other stamps in the Stamp tool menu G.

TIP If you never expect to use your stamp at a large size on the page, you can save some space on your disk by selecting the "Down sample stamp to reduce file size" check box in the Create Custom Stamp dialog F. This option can reduce your stamp's size consid-erably, but it can also make your stamp look chunky if you use the stamp's handles to enlarge it.

TIP You can quickly create a one-off stamp by copying a graphic to the clipboard (in what-ever application you want) and then choosing Paste Clipboard Image As Stamp Tool at the bottom of the Stamp tool menu H.

continues on next page

Having created a custom stamp, you can remove it using the Manage Custom Stamps dialog ❶.

To delete a custom stamp:

1. In the Stamp tool's menu, select Custom Stamps > Manage Stamps.

   Acrobat displays the Manage Custom Stamps dialog.

2. In the list of stamps, select the stamp you want to delete.

   Acrobat shows the stamp's graphic in the dialog.

3. Click Delete.

   Acrobat deletes the custom stamp.

4. Click OK.

TIP As you can see in ❶, you can also edit the selected stamp (rename it and change its category) and create new stamps.

❶ The Manage Custom Stamps dialog lets you delete and edit existing custom stamps and create new ones.

A Use the Check Spelling dialog to check the spelling in comments and form fields.

B When Acrobat finds a misspelled word, it presents you with a list of alternatives.

Checking Spelling in Comments

Acrobat has a built-in spelling checker that looks for spelling errors in a document's comments and form fields. The only difficulty in using this feature is finding it; it's located in a submenu that's otherwise unrelated to forms or commenting.

To check spelling in your comments:

1. Choose Edit > Check Spelling > In Comments, Fields, & Editable Text.

   The Check Spelling dialog opens **A**.

2. Click the Start button.

   Acrobat examines all the comments and form text fields in your document, looking for spelling errors. When it finds a misspelling, Acrobat presents the error in context and shows you a list of replacements **B**.

3. For each misspelled word, do one of the following:

   ▸ Click Ignore to ignore that instance of the misspelled word.

   ▸ Click Ignore All to ignore all instances of that word.

   ▸ Choose a replacement in the list, and click either Change or Change All.

   ▸ Click Add to add the word to Acrobat's dictionary of known words.

   After you change, ignore, or add the misspelled word, Acrobat goes on to the next.

4. When there are no more misspellings, click Done.

Enabling Commenting in Adobe Reader

Adobe Reader X added the ability to apply sticky notes and highlight text in a PDF page. This is useful, because it gives readers the ability to make at least minimal comments on any PDF file.

However, if you want people to be able to review your PDF document in Adobe Reader using the full range of markup tools, you must explicitly turn on that capability for the document, saving it as a *Reader-extended* document.

Once your PDF document has been extended for full commenting in Reader, you're restricted in what else you can do to that document. Even if you're examining the file in Acrobat X, you can no longer shuffle pages, edit page contents, add form fields or links, or otherwise modify the document. This will remain true until you disable Acrobat's ability to annotate the document in Reader.

To enable a document for commenting in Adobe Reader:

1. Choose File > Save as > Reader Extended PDF > Enable Commenting & Measuring.

   Acrobat presents you with a dialog warning you that file editing will be restricted **Ⓐ**. Then a Save dialog opens, because Acrobat insists that you resave the Reader-enabled file.

2. Save the Reader-enabled file with a new name and new location on your disk.

Ⓐ Acrobat warns you that once a document is enabled for commenting in Adobe Reader, editing capabilities are limited, even in Acrobat X.

TIP You can also choose File > Save As > Reader Extended PDF > Enable Additional Features, which will allow Adobe Reader users to apply a digital signature to the document, as well as use all the commenting tools.

Reading Commented Documents

The previous chapter described how to annotate a PDF file with sticky notes, circles, arrows, and paragraphs of explanatory text. In this chapter, we discuss what to do when you receive such a marked-up document. Of course, you can always just double-click an annotation and read the text in the resulting pop-up window. However, Acrobat gives you several more-efficient ways of examining a document's annotations.

Acrobat X's presentation of the list of a document's comments is much improved over previous versions of the software. The list of comments is much more concise, and the process by which you work with those comments—replying, categorizing, searching, and so on—has been greatly streamlined. We now have easy, efficient access to all of the tools we need to examine and work with a document's annotations.

Let's see what those tools are.

Examining the Comments List

The Comments List is a panel in the Comment pane that lists all of the comments in your document . It is invaluable when you're working with a document that has more than just a few comments.

Each entry in the list represents a single comment in your document **B**. The entry supplies a lot of information about the comment, including the name of the commenter, the date the comment was placed on the page, and the comment text.

By default, comments reside in the list in page order and, within each page, by position from top down. Clicking an entry in the Comments List takes you to the comment's page and selects the comment. This means that the easiest way to view all of a document's comments is to simply click each entry in the Comments List, starting at the top of the list and working your way down.

Later in the chapter you'll learn how to change the order of comments within the list.

A The Comments List, in the Comment pane, lists all of the comments in your document.

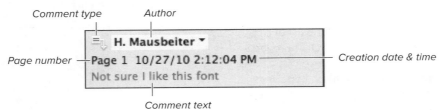

B Each entry in the list supplies information about a single comment in the document.

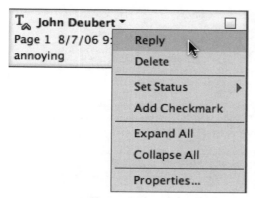

A Right-clicking (Control-clicking) a comment in the Comments List yields a menu with useful commands.

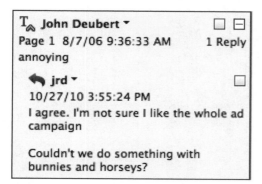

B When you reply to a comment, Acrobat adds your name and the current date to the comment entry in the list and then lets you type in your reply.

C Your reply becomes part of the comment's entry in the Comments List.

Replying to a Comment

Having read a comment, you may want to reply to it, perhaps to answer a question posed in the comment, deny any wrong-doing implied by the comment, and so on.

To reply to a comment in the Comments List:

1. Right-click (Control-click) the comment in the Comments List.

   A short context menu appears with a set of commands you can apply to the comment **A**.

2. Choose Reply from the context menu.

   Acrobat expands the comment's entry in the list, adding your name, the current date, and a text field into which you can type your reply **B**.

3. Type your comment into the list. Press the Tab key or click outside the comment when you are done.

   Acrobat adds the reply to the comment's entry in the list, including your name and the current date **C**.

continues on next page

TIP You can also access the context menu in step **1** by clicking the tiny down arrow visible in 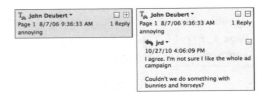**(A)**.

TIP Normally, the Comments List shows only the original comment and an indication of how many replies it has **(D)**. When you click the small "+" box in the upper-right corner of the comment, Acrobat expands the entry, showing all of the replies.

TIP You can toggle the display of all of the replies in all the comments in the list by choosing Expand All or Collapse All in the Options menu at the top of the Comments List **(E)**.

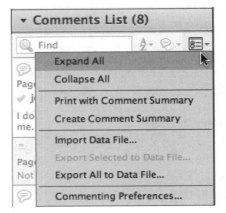

(D) You can show and hide a comment's replies by clicking the little +/- box in the upper-right corner of its list entry.

(E) The Options menu lets you show or hide all of the replies in the Comments List.

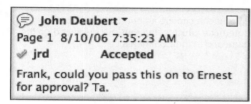

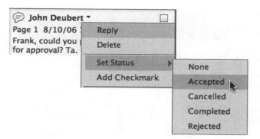

A You can assign a status to a comment by right-clicking (Control-clicking) it in the Comments List.

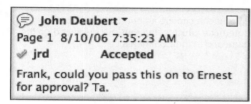

B The status you have chosen here (Accepted) is added with your name to the comment's entry.

C Each comment entry has a check box whose significance is up to you.

Marking Comments

The Comments List lets you indicate that you have reviewed a comment. Setting a comment's review status indicates that you have come to some decision about that comment, such as accepting it as true or rejecting it as an outright and scurrilous lie.

To set the review status of a comment:

1. Right-click (Control-click) the comment in the Comments List.

2. Choose the status you want in the Set Status submenu **A**.

   The comment's new status appears in the Comments List **B**.

TIP Acrobat provides five status values: None, Accepted, Cancelled, Completed, and Rejected. The precise meaning of these status values is up to the reviewer. Acrobat doesn't define the difference between, for example, Cancelled and Rejected.

Each comment in the Comments List has a check box whose significance is up to the reviewer **C**. For example, while reading all the comments in the document, you could check the ones to which you later want to reply.

To set or clear a comment's check mark:

- Click the comment's check box. This action toggles the checked state; it turns on if it was off and vice versa.

TIP You can also mark a comment by right-clicking (Control-clicking) the comment and choosing Set Checkmark. This menu item becomes Remove Checkmark if the comment is already checked.

Managing the Comments List

The set of controls at the top of the Comments List gives you considerable control over which comments it displays and how it displays them. In this section you'll learn how to sort and modify the visibility of items in the Comments List.

The Comments List's Filter menu lets you choose which comments you want to appear on the PDF page and in the list 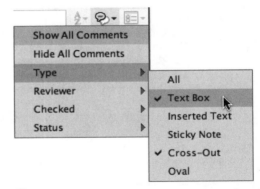. This menu contains a series of submenus that let you specify the visibility of comments by type, reviewer, status, and whether the comment is checked.

Each submenu lets you choose among the available comment types, reviewers, and so on. Note in Ⓐ that you can have multiple selections scattered among the submenus. You can choose to see all the Notes and Text Editing Markups from reviewer Roy G. Biv, for example.

To choose which comments should be visible:

1. In the Comments List toolbar, click the Filter menu Ⓐ.

2. Choose the type, reviewer, status, or checked state you want to make visible in the Comments List.

3. To make all comments visible again, simply choose Show All Comments in the Filter menu.

Ⓐ You can choose among a variety of criteria to determine which comments are displayed on the page and in the Comments List.

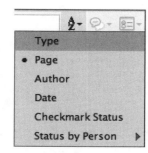

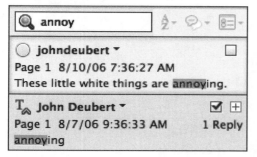

B You can sort the Comments List in several ways.

C The Search field lets you display only those comments that contain a certain word or phrase.

The Comments List toolbar also has a Sort menu that lets you sort the comments in the list by a variety of criteria, including type, page number, and author **B**.

To sort the items in the Comments List:

1. In the Comments List toolbar, click the Sort menu.

2. Choose the criterion by which you want to sort the comments.

   The list immediately redraws itself in the new order.

You can also search for text in the document's comments, displaying only those that contain the desired text.

To search for text in the Comments List:

1. In the Comments List toolbar, click in the Search field **C**.

2. Type the text that you want to find in the comments.

   The list immediately redraws itself, showing only comments that contain the text you are looking for. The found text is highlighted in each of the displayed comments.

Printing Comments

You can print the comments in a document two ways:

- Print the PDF file as usual, with the comments in place on the printed pages.

- Print a summary of the comments, printing the comment text and, optionally, a reduced image of each document page showing where the comment occurs in the document.

To print a PDF file with comments in place:

1. Choose File > Print.

   Acrobat presents you with the Print dialog **A**.

2. In the Comments and Forms pop-up menu **B**, choose one of the following:

   ▸ To print the document and annotations other than stamps, choose Document and Markups.

   ▸ To print the document and stamps, choose Document and Stamps.

   You can't print both markups and stamps; just because.

3. Click Print.

   Acrobat prints the document and annotations.

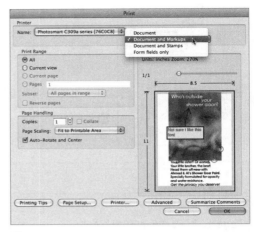

A The Print dialog lets you print your document together with its comments.

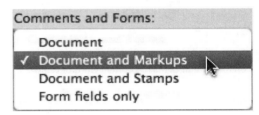

B You can print the document and either its markups or its stamps.

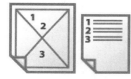

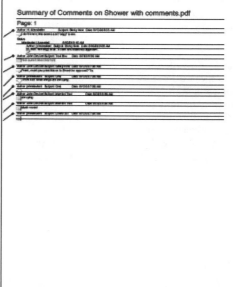

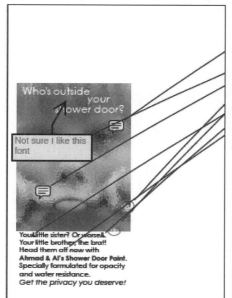

Summarizing Comments

Printing a document with its comments has one serious drawback: Acrobat does not print the annotation text of any comments except text boxes. All the other comment types are printed simply as icons.

Fortunately, Acrobat can also print a summary of all the document's comments; this summary includes the text for all the annotations.

You can choose among four formats for the printed summary **Ⓐ**:

- Each document page alternating with a page of comment text. Lines connect the comment text to the corresponding place on the document page when the pages are placed side by side **Ⓑ**.

continues on next page

Ⓐ Acrobat offers four formats for printing a summary of a document's comments.

Ⓑ Most of the summary formats print each comment's text and indicate its position on the document page.

- A thumbnail of each page printed side by side on a single page with the comment text for that page. Lines connect each comment with the corresponding position on the document page.

- A list of all the comment text, sorted by page number.

- Each document page alternating with a page of comment text. Each comment is numbered, and a corresponding number is placed at the comment's position on the document page.

To print a summary of a document's comments:

1. In the Comments List toolbar, click the Options menu **C**.

2. Choose Create Comment Summary. The Summarize Options dialog opens **D**.

3. Click the radio button corresponding to the type of summary you want.

4. Click the Print Comment Summary button. Acrobat prints the comment summary.

TIP As a convenience, you can choose Print with Comment Summary in the Comments List's Options menu **C** and Acrobat will print a numbered comment summary that is identical to the fourth format listed above. You can also get this same summary by clicking the Summarize Comments button at the bottom of the Print dialog (see **A** in "Printing Comments").

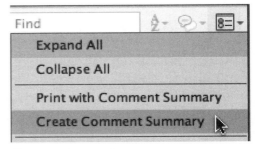

C You print a comment summary from the Comments List's Options menu.

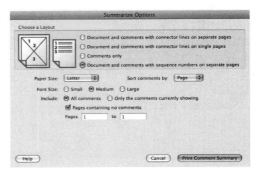

D The Summarize Options dialog lets you select the format you want for the summary.

Reviewing
PDF Documents

In previous chapters we discussed Acrobat's tools for placing and reading comments on a PDF page. The techniques those chapters covered are excellent for soliciting comments from two or three other people.

However, what if you're conducting a company-wide review of a document? You may be sending the PDF file to a dozen people to get comments and critiques; you will need to track your reviewers, who responded, and what they said.

Acrobat X makes it relatively easy to conduct a broadly distributed review of a document. Acrobat manages the process for you, sending copies of the document to reviewers and then collecting all their comments into a single copy of the file.

Acrobat can deliver copies to reviewers in two ways: by arranging a server-based distribution using Acrobat.com or a corporate network (a shared review), or by emailing the document to all the reviewers (an email-based review).

Let's look at how to do both.

Examining the Review Panel

The tools you use to conduct a review of a document all reside in the Review panel of the Comment pane .

This simple pane has four tools:

- **Send for Shared Review** sends the current document for a server-based review using Acrobat.com. Your reviewers must have Acrobat 9 or Adobe Reader 9 or later to review your document.

- **Send for Email Review** emails your document to a list of reviewers. Use this option when some of your recipients have older versions of Acrobat. It is a bit less sophisticated; use a shared review if you can.

- **Collaborate Live** lets you and a collection of reviewers share a document window so you can all discuss the document online. This requires that all the participants be running Acrobat 9 or Adobe Reader 9 or later.

- **Track Reviews** lets you examine the reviews that are in progress, see who has responded, send reminders to people, and so on.

Ⓐ The Review panel in the Comment pane supplies the tools you need to conduct a multiperson review of a document.

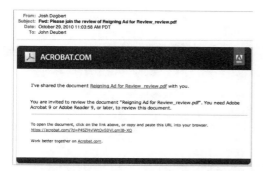

From: Josh Dogbert
Subject: Fwd: Please join the review of Reigning Ad for Review_review.pdf
Date: October 29, 2010 11:03:58 AM PDT
To: John Deubert

ACROBAT.COM

I've shared the document Reigning Ad for Review_review.pdf with you.

You are invited to review the document "Reigning Ad for Review_review.pdf". You need Adobe Acrobat 9 or Adobe Reader 9, or later, to review this document.

To open the document, click on the link above, or copy and paste this URL into your browser.
https://acrobat.com/?d=P4SZHvIWtQvSDVLamIB-XQ

Work better together on Acrobat.com.

A When invited to a shared review, reviewers are emailed a link to the PDF document, which is stored on the Acrobat.com server.

Starting a Shared Review

A shared review is the preferred way of conducting a review among a group of people. It is technically more efficient than an email-based review, because all the comments are stored in a single location rather than being shuttled around attached to different copies of the document.

The disadvantage of a shared review is that it's server-based, so someone must set up and maintain a location on a server to act as a repository for the PDF file, its comments, and the associated bookkeeping. Happily, this is very easy, because Adobe does it for you as part of Acrobat.com.

Chapter 5 discussed Acrobat.com as a file sharing medium. This chapter covers how to use Acrobat.com to distribute and manage review documents.

When you use Acrobat.com for your shared review, Acrobat automatically uploads your PDF file to the Acrobat.com server; Acrobat then emails to all of your reviewers a link to that file on the server **A**. When your reviewers click the link, their copies of Acrobat automatically download the file and open it for review.

Reviewers can then add comments to the file as usual. When finished, reviewers click a Publish Comments button that tells Acrobat to upload the comments back to Acrobat.com.

TIP If you—or your IT department—prefer, you can host the shared review on your own server. I counsel against it unless there's some overwhelming reason. If you have extremely sensitive documents that shouldn't be let loose outside your corporate environment, then it makes sense to host these reviews yourself. Otherwise, Acrobat.com is the way to go; it does a very good job.

To start a shared review:

1. In the Review panel of the Comment pane, select the Send for Shared Review tool.

   Acrobat displays the first pane of the Send for Shared Review Wizard, which records what server you want to use **B**.

2. In the pop-up menu, choose "Automatically download & track comments with Acrobat.com" **C**, and then click Next.

   The pop-up menu also lets you use your own server to collect people's comments; however, someone needs to set up space on a Web- or SMB-based server volume to do this. In this book, we assume you'll be using Acrobat.com, because it's easy, good, and free.

3. If you are not already logged in to Acrobat.com, you are presented with a dialog that lets you do so **D**. Supply your email address and password, and click the Sign In button.

   Note this dialog also lets you create a new Acrobat.com account if you don't already have one. Trust me, you want one of these accounts; the benefits are many and the disadvantages are nil.

   Once you are logged in, Acrobat presents you with the next pane of the Send for Shared Review Wizard **E**, which lets you invite reviewers.

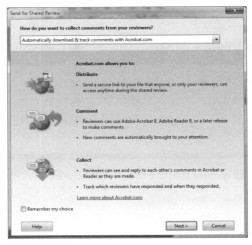

B When starting a shared review, you must first decide where to store the review document and comments.

C The review document and comments can be stored on Acrobat.com or on a Web- or SMB-based server of your choice. Pick Acrobat.com; you'll be happier.

D If you are not already logged in to Acrobat.com, you'll be prompted to do so.

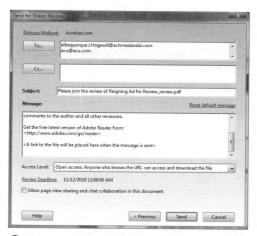

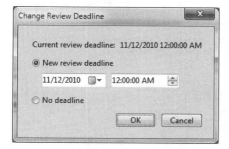

E You can edit the subject and message of the reviewer notification email.

F You must decide who has access to the review document: anyone who knows the address or only people you have specifically notified.

G You can set a deadline for the review; Acrobat.com will not accept comments on the document after this date.

Reigning Ad.pdf   **Reigning Ad_review.pdf**

H Acrobat creates a review copy of the original PDF file. This is the file you will open to see comments sent by reviewers.

4. Type the email addresses of the reviewers into the text box.

   You can separate reviewers' email addresses with spaces, semicolons, or line breaks.

5. Specify an access level for the reviewed document by using the pop-up menu **F**. You can specify that only the people you notify can access the file or that the file can be reviewed by anyone who knows its URL.

   If your document is the least bit sensitive or private, you should make it available only to the people you invite.

6. If you want to set a deadline for the review, click the Review Deadline link and enter a date in the resulting dialog **G**.

7. If you want to use page sharing and chat collaboration with this file, select the "Allow page view sharing and chat collaboration in this document" check box.

   We'll talk about this feature later in the chapter; it's wicked cool.

8. Click Send.

   Acrobat posts the PDF file to the server folder and notifies the reviewers by email. When you are done setting up the shared review, you will find a new copy of your PDF file in the same folder as the original. This new version will have the same filename as the old, with "_review" added **H**. This is the copy of the file that you will use to view reviewers' comments.

Reviewing a Shared Document

If you are on the reviewers list for a shared review, you receive an email that contains a link to the PDF file stored on Acrobat.com 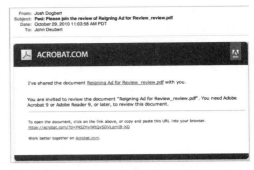. In brief, you retrieve the PDF file from Acrobat.com, add your comments to the file, and then post the comments back to Acrobat.com—all very easy.

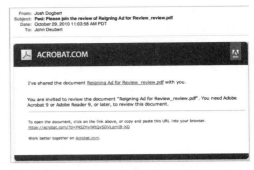

A The link in the notification email leads the reviewer to Acrobat.com where the reviewer can download the file and then open it in Acrobat.

To review a server-based document:

1. In your email software, click the link to the PDF file in the email invitation that was sent to you.

   Acrobat launches your Web browser, taking you to Acrobat.com, which presents you with a Download button **B**.

2. Click the Downloads button in the Acrobat.com window.

   Acrobat downloads the review copy of the document to your hard disk.

3. Open the document.

   The file opens with an extra toolbar added to the top of the document window **C**. Each document page shows the comments already placed there by other reviewers.

4. Add your comments, using the comment tools as usual.

5. Click the Publish Comments button at the top of the document window **D**.

   Acrobat stores your comments on the Acrobat.com server.

> **TIP** You can check to see if any new comments have been added to the reviewed document by clicking the Check for New Comments button in the review toolbar **C**.

B Acrobat.com lets the reviewer download the file to a local disk for markup.

C When the review document is opened on the reviewer's computer, Acrobat adds a toolbar to the top of the document window.

D When the reviewer is finished annotating the document, the PDF file publishes those comments back to Acrobat.com when the Publish Comments button is clicked.

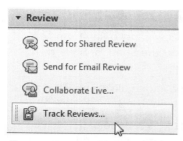

A Display the Tracker window by selecting the Track Reviews tool in the Comment pane's Review panel.

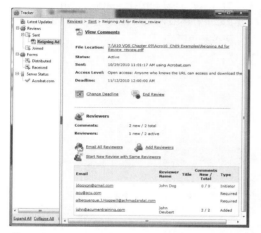

B Clicking a shared review in the Tracker window displays a list of reviewers and other information about that review.

TIP There are many other things you can do through the Review Tracker, including starting a new review using the same set of reviewers and sending an email to one or all of the reviewers.

Receiving Server-based Reviews

The best way to collect comments from a shared review is to use the Acrobat Review Tracker. This tool lists all the reviews you've initiated and lets you conveniently see the current state of all their comments.

To read comments from a server-based review:

1. In the Review panel of the Comment pane, select the Track Reviews tool **A**.

   Acrobat presents you with the Tracker window **B**. This window lets you track all current reviews, whether email-based or shared, as well as results returned from people filling out PDF format forms.

2. In the left pane, click the review you want to examine (Reigning Ad in **B**).

   The right side of the window shows information about that review, such as when the emailed invitations were sent, who the reviewers are, and so on.

3. Click the View Comments link (near the top of the right pane).

   Acrobat opens the review copy of the PDF file, displaying all the comments made by the various reviewers.

4. View the comments in the document as discussed in Chapter 8.

TIP You can reply to comments in your shared review and publish the replies back to Acrobat.com by clicking the document's Publish Comments button, as covered in the previous section of this chapter. Your reviewers will all be able to see your replies.

Real-time Collaborative Reviews

Real-time live collaboration was introduced in Acrobat 9, and a stunning feature it is, too. If you enable this for a particular shared review, reviewers can participate in a live chat within Acrobat, discussing the document online. It is even possible for one of the reviewers to share his or her screen with the other online reviewers, so that everyone is looking at the same document view as the discussion proceeds.

This is very cool stuff, particularly because it is available to anyone reviewing the document with Acrobat and Adobe Reader 9 or X.

Live collaboration is enabled on a review-by-review basis.

To enable live collaboration:

1. In the Review panel of the Comment pane, select the Send for Shared Review tool.

   Supply the information requested by the resulting Wizard.

2. In the Wizard's second panel, select the "Allow page view sharing and chat collaboration in this document" 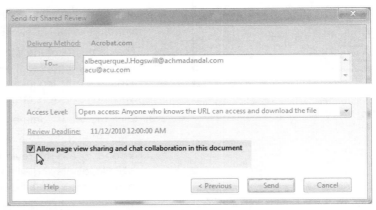 check box.

   That's it; real-time collaboration is available to all the reviewers of this document.

A You allow a review document to be used in live collaboration by selecting the check box "Allow page view sharing and chat collaboration in this document."

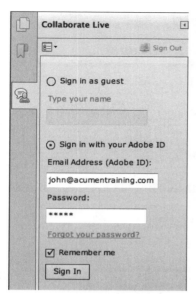

Collaborate Live

☰ ▾   Sign Out

○ Sign in as guest
Type your name

⊙ Sign in with your Adobe ID
Email Address (Adobe ID):
john@acumentraining.com
Password:
*****
Forgot your password?
☑ Remember me
Sign In

B When you open a document that is enabled for live collaboration, Acrobat automatically displays the Collaborate Live navigation pane.

To use live collaboration:

1. Open a document that has been enabled for live collaboration.

   Acrobat displays the Collaborate Live navigation pane along the left side of the screen **B**.

2. Sign in to Acrobat.com using the email address and password fields in the Collaborate Live pane, and then click the Sign In button.

   This pane reconfigures itself, displaying a list of currently online reviewers and a basic e-chat facility **C**.

3. Conduct your discussion in typical text chat style. Just type text in the Document Chat field at the bottom of the pane and press the Enter (Return) key or click Send. Your text immediately appears in the other reviewers' Collaborate Live panes.

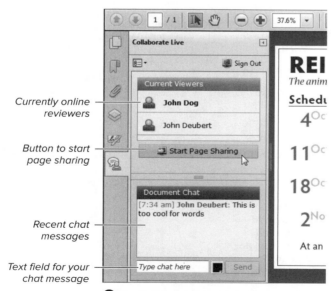

Currently online reviewers

Button to start page sharing

Recent chat messages

Text field for your chat message

C The Collaborate Live navigation pane has a list of online reviewers, a simple but effective chat interface, and a button that starts live page sharing.

Page sharing

Anyone who has collaborated on a document with someone who lives or works in a different location knows what a nuisance it can be to discuss that document over the telephone. Trying to get the other person to understand which item on the page it is that bothers you can take years off your life in frustration. Enter page sharing.

During a live collaboration session, you can turn on page sharing and every online reviewer will see exactly what you see: Their copies of Acrobat display the same document page as yours; when you change pages, automatically, theirs do as well. As long as page sharing is enabled, their view of the document will be slaved to yours ❶.

I cannot adequately tell you how exciting this is for those of us who routinely work on documents with other people!

To initiate page sharing:

1. Initiate a live collaboration session, as described in the previous section.

2. Click the Start Page Sharing button ❸.

One minor but cool feature while page sharing is active is that everyone gets to see where everyone else's mouse pointers are on the page; each reviewer's pointer appears as a small arrow, identified by the reviewer's name ❹.

TIP Page sharing disables any tools that modify the page contents. You cannot edit text or objects, and although you can add comments to the page, the comments are not visible to the people sharing the page. Page sharing is intended to be a discussion tool, not a group editing tool.

❶ When page sharing is turned on, all the online reviewers see the same view of the document as you do.

❹ All the reviewers' pointers are visible when page sharing is turned on; each is identified with the reviewer's name.

Starting an Email-based Review

Server-based reviews and live collaboration require that all your reviewers have at least Acrobat 9 installed on their computers. Sometimes you can't be sure this is the case; it's surprisingly hard to ensure that everyone has a reasonably recent version of Acrobat, especially if your stable of reviewers is very large. In this case, you will need to conduct an email-based review.

In an email-based review, Acrobat emails copies of your document to a group of reviewers you designate. When your reviewers open the document, they comment on it using the standard Acrobat annotation tools and then return the document by email. When you open each returned, annotated copy, Acrobat merges the comments into your original PDF file. Eventually, the original file will contain the comments returned by all the reviewers.

Reviewers can respond to an email-based review if they have Acrobat 6 or Adobe Reader 7 or later. People running versions older than these are probably not able to operate keyboards, either, so they wouldn't be useful reviewers in any case.

TIP Keep in mind that most email servers have a limit to attachment size, usually 5 MB or so. If your PDF file is bigger than this, you won't be able to use an email-based review; server-based reviews do not have any restriction on file size.

To start an email-based review:

1. In the Review panel of the Comment pane, select the Send for Email Review tool.

   Acrobat displays the first step in the Email-Based Review Wizard, which gives an overview of the process and selects the file for review **Ⓐ**.

2. Click the Choose button, and select the PDF file to be reviewed in the pick-a-file dialog.

   You could also select an open PDF document from the pop-up menu.

3. Click Next.

   Acrobat displays the second step in the Email-Based Review Wizard, which allows you to invite reviewers **Ⓑ**.

4. Type the email addresses of your reviewers into the text box.

   You can separate reviewers' email addresses with spaces, semicolons, or new lines.

   Alternatively, you can click the Address Book button and choose people in your system's address book.

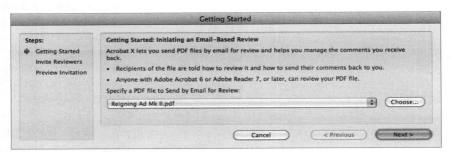

Ⓐ The first step in the Email-Based Review Wizard specifies the file that is to be reviewed.

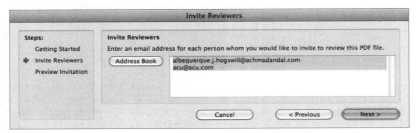

Ⓑ The second step in the Wizard collects the email addresses of all your reviewers.

5. Click Next.

Acrobat displays the final step in the Wizard, which lets you read and modify the email the reviewers will see **C**.

6. Type the text you want for your email's subject in the Preview Invitation's Subject field.

7. Modify or replace the email's message text as desired in the Preview Invitation's Message field.

In most cases, you should leave the message text as is, because it provides detailed directions to the reviewers on what to do.

8. Click the Send Invitation button.

Acrobat launches your email client and displays the outbound message with the PDF file attached **D**.

9. Click your email client's Send button or otherwise send the email message on its way.

TIP Depending on your computer setup, you may not see your email client. In particular, the Windows version of Acrobat may send the email messages directly.

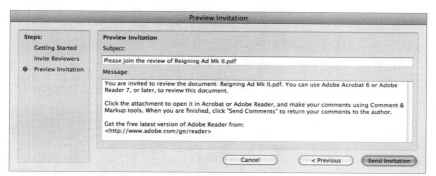

C You finish by editing the subject and message text of the notification emails.

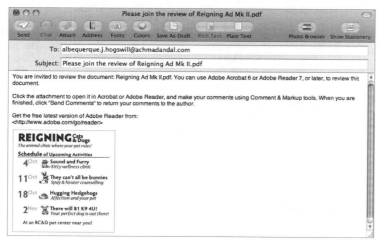

D When you're invited to review a document, the PDF file is attached to the emailed notification.

Reviewing an Emailed Document

When you receive a document for review, you get an email with the PDF file attached. When you open the attached PDF file, Acrobat recognizes that it's part of a review and adds an extra toolbar to the top of the document window **Ⓐ**. This toolbar has brief instructions as to what to do with the file and a Send Comments button.

To review a PDF document:

1. Open the PDF file attached to the notification email.

   If another reviewer sent you this email, Acrobat presents you with the Merge Comments dialog, which asks if you want to see the other people's comments **Ⓑ**.

2. If you are presented with the Merge Comments dialog, click Yes or "No, open this copy only," according to whether you want to see other people's comments.

   Acrobat displays the document in a window with the added toolbar **Ⓐ**.

3. Make your comments on the document, as described in Chapter 7.

4. When you're finished annotating the document, click the Send Comments button.

   The Send Comments dialog opens **Ⓒ**.

5. Click the Send button.

   Acrobat launches your email client and displays the outbound message with the PDF file attached.

6. Click your email client's Send button or otherwise send the email message on its way.

Ⓐ Acrobat presents the reviewer with instructions on how to review the emailed document and a Send Comments button.

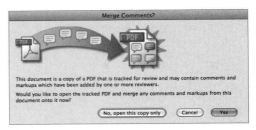

Ⓑ When a reviewer opens the email attachment, Acrobat offers to display any comments placed in the file by other reviewers.

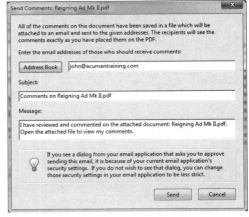

Ⓒ When the reviewer clicks Send Comments, Acrobat provides a chance to alter the return email's subject and message texts.

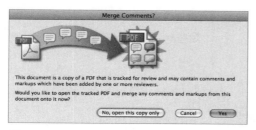

A When the author opens a reviewed copy of the document, Acrobat offers to merge the comments into the original PDF file.

Receiving Email-reviewed Documents

When you receive a reviewed copy of your document, the annotated version of the PDF file is attached to the notification email. Open this attached document, and Acrobat merges the comments it contains into your original copy.

To receive a reviewed document:

1. From your email software, open the attached PDF file in Acrobat X.

    Acrobat presents you with the Merge Comments dialog **A**, which asks if you want to merge the comments into your copy of the document.

2. Click the Yes button.

    Acrobat opens the original PDF document and imports the comments from the attached PDF file into your original.

3. Read the comments as described in Chapter 8.

Manipulating Pages

Acrobat X provides tools that make it easy to insert, delete, rearrange, and otherwise change the order of pages within a PDF document.

You can access these features in three ways:

- Select a tool in the Pages panel of the Tools pane **Ⓐ**.

- Right-click (Control-click) a thumbnail in the Page Thumbnails navigation pane **Ⓑ**. Acrobat displays a context menu that contains all the page-manipulation commands.

- Click the Options button at the top of the Page Thumbnails navigation pane **Ⓒ**. This yields the same menu as when you right-click (Control-click) a thumbnail.

I find it most convenient to right-click (Control-click) pages in the Page Thumbnails navigation pane, although I have moods when I frequent the Pages panel.

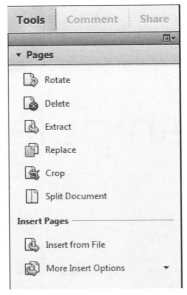

Ⓐ The tools for manipulating pages can be found in the Pages panel of the Tools pane.

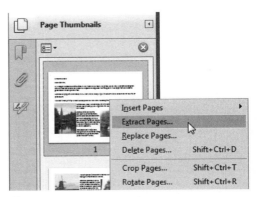

Ⓑ You can also manipulate pages by right-clicking (Control-clicking) a page in the Page Thumbnails navigation pane.

Ⓒ And, finally, you can access the tools by clicking the Options menu at the top of the Page Thumbnails navigation pane.

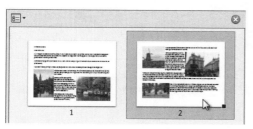

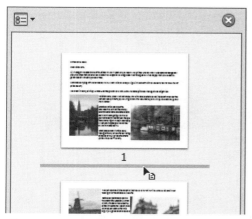

Rearranging Pages

You can move pages around in a PDF file using the Page Thumbnails navigation pane . Simply drag pages from their original locations to the places you want them.

To move a page from one location to another:

1. Click the Page Thumbnails navigation tab (at the left of the document window) to open the Page Thumbnails navigation pane.

   Acrobat displays thumbnails of all the document pages.

2. Click the thumbnail of the page you want to move.

   Acrobat creates a dark background around the thumbnail, indicating that the page is selected **B**.

3. Drag the selected thumbnail to its new position in the document.

   As you drag the page, Acrobat places a light-colored line between existing thumbnails, indicating where the page will be placed **C**.

4. Release the mouse button.

   Acrobat moves the selected page to its new location.

A The Page Thumbnails navigation pane makes it easy to rearrange the pages in your document.

B When you select a thumbnail in the Page Thumbnails pane, Acrobat highlights the thumbnail with a dark background.

C As you drag a page in the Page Thumbnails navigation pane, a gray line indicates the page's new location.

TIP You can select more than one thumbnail in the Page Thumbnails pane. Acrobat follows the conventional mouse-click rules: Shift-click selects a range of thumbnails; Ctrl-click (Command-click) selects a noncontiguous set of pages.

Extracting Pages

You can extract a range of pages from a PDF file and create a new PDF file from those pages. Acrobat can extract the pages into a single PDF file or create a separate PDF file for each page.

To extract a range of pages from a document:

1. In the Pages panel of the Tools pane, choose the Extract tool **A**.

    Acrobat presents you with the Extract Pages dialog **B**.

2. In the From and To fields, indicate the beginning and ending page numbers of the pages you want to extract.

3. If you want to remove those pages from the original document, select the check box Delete Pages After Extracting.

4. If you want each extracted page to become a separate, one-page PDF document, select the check box Extract Pages As Separate Files.

5. Click OK.

    Acrobat extracts the pages as you've specified. The extracted pages appear in a new window named "Pages from [original document].pdf."

TIP As an alternative, you can select a set of thumbnails in the Page Thumbnails navigation pane, right-click (Control-click) one of the selected thumbnails, and choose Extract Pages from the context menu. The Extract Pages dialog opens with the page range already set to the pages you selected.

A The Extract tool resides in the Pages panel of the Tools pane.

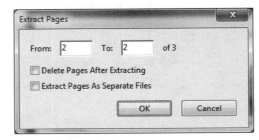

B In the Extract Pages dialog, you specify the range of pages you want to extract.

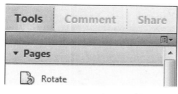

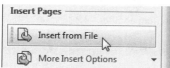

A To insert pages into the current document, select the Insert from File tool.

B The Insert Pages dialog lets you specify where the inserted pages should be placed.

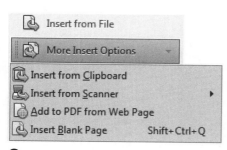

C The More Insert Options submenu in the Pages panel lets you insert a variety of other items into your document.

Inserting One File into Another

Acrobat makes it easy to insert the contents of another PDF file into your current document.

To insert pages from another file into a document:

1. In the Pages panel of the Tools pane, choose the Insert from File tool **A**.

   The standard Open dialog opens.

2. Choose the file that contains the pages you want to insert, and click OK.

   Acrobat presents you with the Insert Pages dialog **B**.

3. Specify where in your document you want the new pages to be inserted.

   Using the Location pop-up menu and the radio buttons, you can select before or after the first page or last page, or a specific page number.

4. Click OK.

   Acrobat inserts the contents of the other file into your current document.

TIP The More Insert Options submenu in the Pages panel lets you insert other items as pages into the PDF file **C**, including Web pages and the clipboard contents. This works exactly like the Create PDF File options discussed in Chapter 2: The selected item is converted to PDF and is immediately inserted into the current document.

Replacing Pages

Acrobat lets you replace a range of pages in the current document with pages taken from another PDF file.

To replace pages in your document:

1. In the Pages panel of the Tools pane, choose the Replace tool 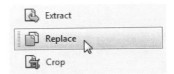.

   The standard Open dialog opens.

2. Select the file that contains the replacement pages, and click OK.

   The Replace Pages dialog opens **B**.

3. In the Original section, specify the range of pages that should be replaced.

4. In the Replacement section, specify the starting page number of the replacement pages in the other PDF file.

   You don't need to specify an ending page number; the length of the replacement page range matches the number of pages you're replacing.

5. Click OK.

   Acrobat replaces the specified pages with pages taken from the other document.

> **TIP** Interestingly, when you replace a range of pages in a document, this does *not* replace any links, comments, or form fields on the original pages. Those remain in place, resting in a layer on top of the new pages. These active elements may not align with anything in particular in the inserted pages; you can select them and remove them with the Delete key.

A The Replace tool lets you replace pages in your document with pages taken from another.

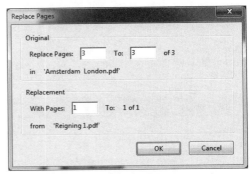

B In the Replace Pages dialog, you indicate which pages should be replaced and which pages in the other document should replace them.

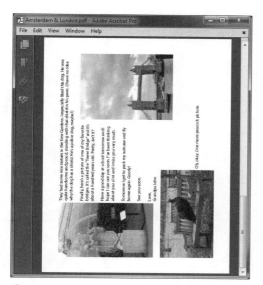

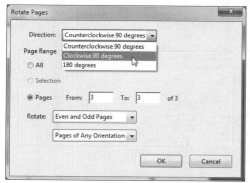

A Many applications produce landscape pages that Acrobat displays in portrait orientation.

B The Rotate Pages dialog lets you specify which pages should be rotated and in what direction they should rotate.

Rotating Pages

When you export a landscape-oriented document from page-layout software or a word processor, Acrobat often displays the resulting pages sideways **A**. The page is laid out in landscape, but Acrobat displays it in portrait orientation.

This is easily fixed by having Acrobat rotate the pages in your document. Acrobat can rotate all the pages or a specified range of pages.

The pages retain their new orientation in future viewings.

To rotate pages in the current document:

1. In the Pages panel of the Tools pane, choose the Rotate Pages tool.

   The Rotate Pages dialog opens **B**.

   In the Direction pop-up menu, choose whether the pages should be rotated 90 degrees clockwise or counterclockwise, or a full 180 degrees.

2. Click the appropriate radio button to choose the range of pages you want to rotate:

   ▸ To rotate the entire document, click All.

   ▸ To rotate pages you've selected in the Page Thumbnails navigation pane, click Selection.

   ▸ To rotate a specific range of page numbers, click Pages, and specify the beginning and ending page numbers.

continues on next page

3. In the Rotate pop-up menu, choose whether you want to rotate even pages, odd pages, or both.

4. In the unnamed pop-up menu below the Rotate pop-up menu, choose whether to rotate landscape pages, portrait pages, or both.

5. Click OK.

   Acrobat rotates the pages you specified **C**.

TIP Acrobat often uses the orientation of text on a page to determine whether that page is landscape or portrait. If you select a specific orientation in step 4, pages with no text on them may not be rotated regardless of the actual orientation of the page.

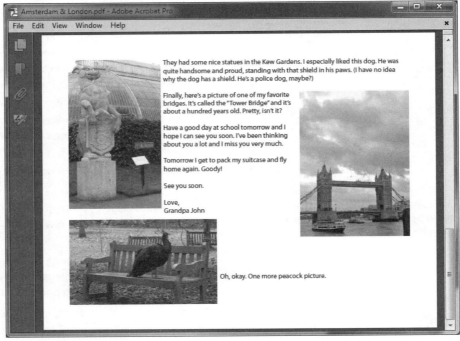

C In Acrobat you can rotate your pages so they are oriented the way you want.

A Many graphics applications produce PDF pages with a lot of white space around the graphic.

B You can crop pages so they display only the part that is useful.

C Having dragged out your crop area, Acrobat displays it with handles at the corners so you can adjust its size.

Cropping Pages

Graphics applications often create PDF files whose pages have a lot of white space around the pages' contents **A**. Acrobat lets you pare down the document page, cropping it so it contains only the content you want **B**. You can also change the page dimensions to a standard size, such as Letter or A4.

To crop a page in a document:

1. With the document open to the page you want to crop, select the Crop tool in the Pages panel.

    The cursor turns into a crosshair.

2. Drag out the rectangular area to which you want to crop the page.

    Acrobat displays a rectangle indicating the area you have chosen **C**.

3. Reposition the rectangle by dragging it around the page, and resize it by dragging the handles at its corners until it is just as you want it.

    Don't obsess over precision at this point; you will have a chance to tweak it in the next couple of steps.

continues on next page

4. Double-click the clip rectangle.

   Acrobat presents you with the Set Page Boxes dialog 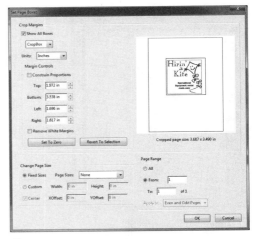. In addition to the page-cropping controls, this dialog has a preview that shows the border of the cropped document.

5. In the Margin Controls section, either enter values for the top, bottom, left, and right margins or click the up and down arrows to increase or decrease the values of these margins **E**.

   As you do so, Acrobat draws a rectangle showing you the present size of the page.

6. In the Page Range section, indicate the range of pages whose size you want to change.

   You can select a range of pages or click All to crop all the pages. By default, the page range is set to include only the current page.

7. Click OK.

   Acrobat reduces the page size.

TIP Acrobat doesn't discard any page content when it crops a page; it simply hides it from view. If you select the cropped page and return to the Set Page Boxes dialog, you can click the Set to Zero button to recover the original page size. This is true even after you have saved, closed, and later reopened the file.

TIP You can choose whichever unit of measure you want from the Units pop-up menu. It offers points, picas, millimeters, centimeters, and inches. No furlongs, I'm afraid. You can also indicate units of measure for the margins by using abbreviations (pt, p, mm, cm, in) in the margin size boxes **E**.

D The Set Page Boxes dialog lets you specify how much of the page should be trimmed from the top, bottom, left, and right of the page.

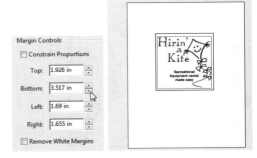

E As you change the margin sizes, Acrobat displays a rectangle in the preview picture, indicating the new page boundaries.

TIP You can use the Set Page Boxes dialog to change the paper size of your document. Select the paper size (Letter, Legal, A4, and so on) from the Page Sizes pop-up menu. I often use this with scanned document pages, which never seem to come out exactly 8.5 by 11 inches. I choose Letter for the page size and all my pages are resized.

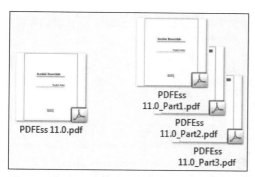

A Acrobat can split your document into smaller, successively named pieces.

Splitting a Document

Sometimes you need to split a document into a series of smaller documents. For example, mail servers usually have a limit (typically 5 MB or so) to the size of attachment files; if you need to email a very large document to someone, your server may not let you. In this case, you'll need to split the document into smaller pieces that won't provoke your mail server's ire.

Acrobat will do this for you with only minimal effort on your part: Just specify the maximum size or number of pages you want in each of the fragments, and Acrobat will produce a set of PDF files derived from the original **A**.

You can specify the file be split in one of three ways:

- Each piece will have up to a specified number of pages.

- Each piece will be not more than a specified number of megabytes in size.

- Each piece will represent a top-level bookmark within the original document; this can make it easy to split a long book into chapter-length sections, for example. (See Chapter 12 for a discussion of bookmarks.)

To split a document into smaller pieces:

1. In the Pages panel, select the Split Document tool.

   Acrobat displays the Split Document dialog 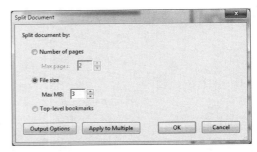.

2. Select the radio button corresponding to how the document should be split: maximum pages, maximum file size, or top-level bookmarks.

3. Click OK.

   Acrobat will split the file as you specified.

TIP The Output Options button lets you specify how the fragments should be named and where they should be placed. By default, the fragments have the same name as the original file with "Part *n*" appended **A**; the fragments are placed in the same folder as the original. I've never found any reason to change these default settings.

TIP The Apply to Multiple button lets you specify a list of files, all of which will be split according to your specification.

B The Split Document dialog lets you specify how your document should be divided: by page count, file size, or top-level bookmarks.

Adding and Changing Text and Graphics

PDF isn't intended to be an editable document format. Adobe meant a PDF file to be a snapshot of a document as it was at a particular time.

Nonetheless, Acrobat breaks with that vision by providing extremely useful tools for touching up a document, making common changes that are convenient to some people and absolutely vital to others. This includes fixing typos, adding page numbers, and even modifying images using Adobe Photoshop or another editor of your choice.

continues on next page

In This Chapter

We'll examine two groups of tools in this chapter, both of which help you modify the contents of a PDF document:

- The **touch-up tools** let you make minor modifications to images, line art, and images on the page. These tools reside in the Content panel of the Tools pane.

- The **page design tools** let you add page elements: headers, footers, a background image, or a watermark. These live in the Pages panel of the Tools pane.

All of these tools have become a bit easier to use in Acrobat X. Let's take a look.

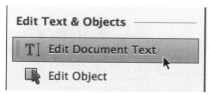

A You touch up text in your PDF file by selecting Edit Document Text in the Content panel of the Tools pane.

B When the Edit Document Text tool is active, you can select text on the PDF page.

Touching Up Text

One of the first—and most requested— editing features Adobe added to Acrobat was the ability to make minor changes to the text in a PDF file. This capability isn't intended for wholesale rewriting of text; rather, it lets you make small changes like fixing a wrong telephone number or adding a missing comma. Before Adobe added this feature, even a minor typo would send you back to your original word-processor file, where you'd have to make the change and regenerate the PDF file.

The Edit Document Text tool resides in the Content panel of the Tools pane **A**. When you select this tool, the pointer becomes a text-editing I-beam whenever it roams over text **B**. You edit text using the same techniques you use in a text editor: Click the text you want to change, and then type your addition or replacement.

To change text in a document:

1. Click the Edit Document Text tool in the Content panel **A**.

2. Either click the text to insert a change or select text that you want to delete or replace.

   Acrobat inserts a blinking cursor at the place you clicked or highlights the text you selected **B**.

3. Type the text you want to insert into the PDF file.

TIP Acrobat implements all the common key commands for moving the blinking cursor to the next word, the end of the line, and so on.

TIP To replace or add text, that text's font must be installed in your computer system.

In addition to inserting and deleting text, the Edit Document Text tool lets you change the font, size, alignment, and other properties of text in your PDF file.

To change text properties:

1. Select the Edit Document Text tool in the Content panel.

2. Select the text whose properties you want to change.

   Right-click (Control-click) the text to display a context menu **C**.

3. Choose Properties.

   Acrobat presents you with the TouchUp Properties dialog **D**.

4. Choose a font from the pop-up menu.

5. If you select a font, also select the Embed and Subset check boxes.

   These options embed the font in the PDF file, ensuring that the text will look the same on other computers.

6. Type a font size into the Font Size field, or select a font size from the pop-up menu next to the field **E**.

7. Click Close.

TIP The TouchUp Properties dialog lets you change a number of other text characteristics, including word spacing and horizontal offset. These can be occasionally useful for adjusting the appearance of your text.

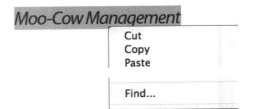

C Right-clicking (Control-clicking) text with the Edit Document Text tool yields a context menu with access to text properties.

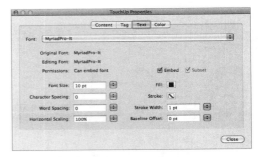

D The TouchUp Properties dialog lets you change the font, size, and other characteristics of the selected text.

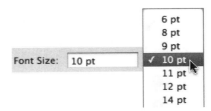

E The Font Size pop-up menu lets you select a predefined point size for the selected text.

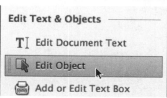

A The Edit Object tool lets you modify line art and images on the PDF page.

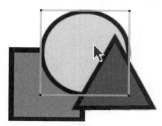

B A bounding rectangle shows that you've selected an object with the Edit Object tool.

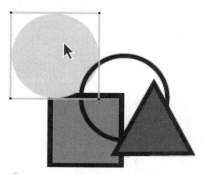

C You can drag objects around the page with the Edit Object tool. Note that the fill and border of an object are often separate.

Modifying Line Art

There are two ways you can change lines, rectangles, and other line art on a PDF page. Acrobat's Edit Object tool lets you change the position and orientation of graphic objects on the page. For extensive changes, Acrobat lets you edit page contents in Adobe Illustrator or another graphics editor.

Keep in mind we're talking about graphic objects that are part of the page content, not the lines, rectangles, and other graphics associated with comments.

Let's first look at Acrobat's built-in tool.

To change an object's position and size:

1. Click the Edit Object tool in the Content panel of the Tools pane **A**.

2. Click a graphic object on the document.

   Acrobat draws a rectangle around the object to indicate that it's selected **B**.

3. To change the object's size, click and drag one of the handles at the corners.

4. To reposition the object, click and drag it to the desired position **C**.

TIP Holding down the Shift key as you drag an object constrains your motion to angles of 90 degrees from the original position.

TIP When you resize an object, Acrobat normally preserves the object's original shape, scaling the object identically in the horizontal and vertical directions. To release this constraint, hold down the Shift key while you drag the object's handles; Acrobat lets you drag that handle anywhere you want, scaling the horizontal and vertical dimensions separately.

Right-clicking (Control-clicking) a graphic object with the Edit Object tool yields a context menu that lets you make a remarkable range of additional changes to the object **D**: flip or rotate the object; replace the existing image with another on your hard disk; and open the object in Illustrator, Photoshop, or other external editor (see below). Simply choose the appropriate command from the menu. These menu commands are generally straightforward; one action that can be unexpectedly tricky is rotating by an arbitrary amount.

To rotate an object by an arbitrary amount:

1. Click the Edit Object tool in the Content panel of the Tools pane.

2. Click a graphic object to select it. Note that if the object consists of separate fill and border objects, you need to select both by dragging a marquee.

3. Right-click (Control-click) the object to access its context menu.

4. Choose Rotate Selection.

5. Click and drag the selection rectangle's corners to rotate the object **E**.

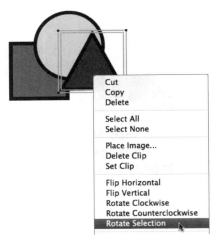

D To rotate artwork on the PDF page, right-click (Control-click) an object and choose Rotate Selection. Note that there are a variety of other commands available.

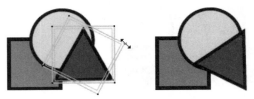

E Having chosen Rotate Selection, you can drag one of the handles at the bounding box's corners to rotate the object.

Selecting Fill and Border

A graphic object can reside in a PDF file as two objects, one each for the fill and the border. In that case, the Edit Object tool may choose only one of the two objects.

If that is the case for the object you're editing, you need to either move the two objects separately or choose both at once by dragging out a marquee with the Edit Object tool **F**. This marquee must touch the outline of the object to choose both the fill and border; it doesn't need to completely enclose the object. Then you can move or resize both the fill and the border of the object.

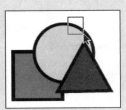

F To choose both the fill and border of an object, with the Edit Object tool, drag a marquee that intersects the object's border.

G You can do anything you wish to PDF artwork you've opened in Illustrator; here we've added eyes and a smile to the circle.

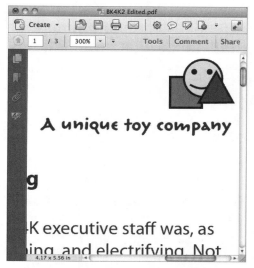

H When you save the artwork from Illustrator, the modified objects are inserted into the original PDF file.

Editing Images

The Edit Object tool works with pixel-based images exactly as it does with line art.

Alt (Option)-double-clicking an image (or selecting Edit Object from the context menu) opens that image in Adobe Photoshop, allowing you to make any change you want to that image. Saving the image from Photoshop inserts the modified image back into the original PDF file.

Editing in Adobe Illustrator

Acrobat also lets you edit graphics in Adobe Illustrator. This capability opens up a vast array of editing possibilities. The cool part is that when you save the modified graphic in Illustrator, it's inserted back into the PDF file. I get excited about this feature! (Why, yes, I do have a simple social life.)

To edit artwork in Illustrator:

1. Click the Edit Object tool in the Content panel of the Tools pane.

2. Do either of the following:
   ▸ While holding down the Alt (Option) key, double-click the artwork.
   ▸ Right-click (Control-click) the object, and choose Edit Object.

   Acrobat launches Illustrator and opens the artwork in a new Illustrator window.

3. Edit the artwork using the usual Illustrator tools.

   You can do anything that is valid in Illustrator, including adding new artwork or text. (The eyes and smile in **G** were added in Illustrator.)

4. In Illustrator, choose File > Save. Illustrator saves the artwork directly into the original PDF file **H**.

TIP Acrobat's Preferences allow you to use alternative editors instead of Illustrator and Photoshop. Go to the Preferences dialog, and choose the Touch Up category. You'll see a pair of controls that let you choose editing software for graphics and images.

Adding Headers and Footers

Acrobat lets you add headers and footers to a PDF file. This new text can be in any font and point size, and can include page numbers and the current date.

The Add Header and Footer dialog, although complex, isn't as confusing as it may seem at first **Ⓐ**.

Note that the header and footer each have three text fields, corresponding to left justified, centered, and right justified. You may supply up to three pieces of text for both the header and the footer, one snippet of text for each of the three positions.

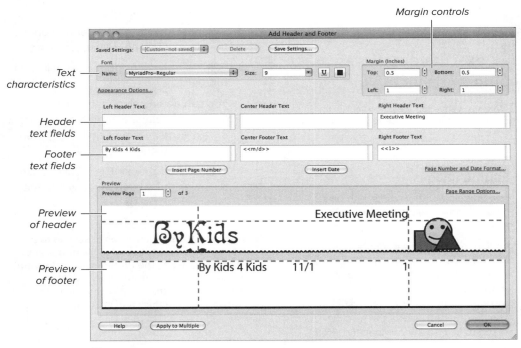

Ⓐ Here are the main sets of controls in the Add Header and Footer dialog.

B You add, change, or remove a header or footer by choosing the appropriate item from the Header & Footer submenu.

C Clicking the Page Range Options link yields this dialog, which lets you specify the pages to which your headers and footers should be applied.

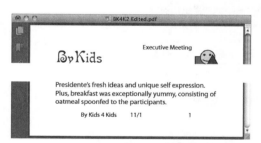

D When you close the Add Header and Footer dialog, your new text appears at the top and bottom of your PDF pages.

To add a header or footer to a document:

1. In the Pages panel of the Tools pane, choose Header & Footer > Add Header & Footer **B**.

   The Add Header and Footer dialog opens **A**.

2. Choose the font and size you want for your header and footer text.

   The controls to the right of the Size combo box let you turn on underlining and specify a text color.

3. In the Margin fields, type the values you want for the top, bottom, left, and right margins.

   The top margin is the baseline for the header; the footer is placed just below the bottom margin.

4. In the six text fields running across the center of the dialog, type the left-justified, centered, and right-justified text for the header and/or footer.

   The preview across the bottom of the dialog shows what your text will look like in place on your document page.

   At any time while typing text, you can click the Insert Page Number button or the Insert Date button to insert the respective value into your text.

5. If you want your header and footer to apply only to certain pages in your document, click the Page Range Options link.

   Acrobat opens a dialog that lets you specify the pages to which the header and footer should be applied **C**.

6. Click OK.

   Acrobat adds the header and footer to your document **D**.

continues on next page

TIP If you have a header and footer combination that you use frequently, you can save your settings by clicking the Save Settings button at the top of the Add Header and Footer dialog **E**. You're asked to name the collection of settings; that name will appear in the Saved Settings pop-up menu.

TIP You can control the appearance of the page number and date inserted into your text. Click the Page Number and Date Format link to the right of the Insert Date button. Acrobat opens a dialog that lets you select from a set of predefined formats **F**.

TIP You can modify your header and footer settings by choosing Header & Footer > Update from the Pages panel. The Add Header and Footer dialog opens, filled in with your current settings. Make whatever changes you want, and click OK.

TIP You can modify an existing header and footer by choosing Header & Footer > Update in the Pages panel.

TIP You can delete your header and footer by choosing Header & Footer > Remove in the Pages panel.

E The Save Settings button lets you add the current set of control settings to the Saved Settings pop-up menu.

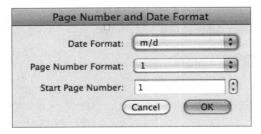

F Clicking the Page Number and Date Format link lets you specify how the page numbers and date will appear on the page.

Tools Comment Share

▾ **Pages**

📄 Rotate

Edit Page Design

⬜ Header & Footer ▾

▨ Background ▾

> Add Background... ▾
> Update...
> Remove... ▾

Ⓐ You add, change, or remove a page's background by choosing the appropriate item from the Background submenu.

Adding a Background

Acrobat can add a background to the pages in your document. That background can be either a solid color or page contents taken from another PDF or image file. In the latter case, the page contents can be any combination of text or graphics.

To add a background to your document pages:

1. In the Pages panel of the Tools pane, choose Background > Add Background Ⓐ.

   The Add Background dialog opens Ⓑ.

2. If you want to use a page from another PDF file as your background, click the File radio button.

continues on next page

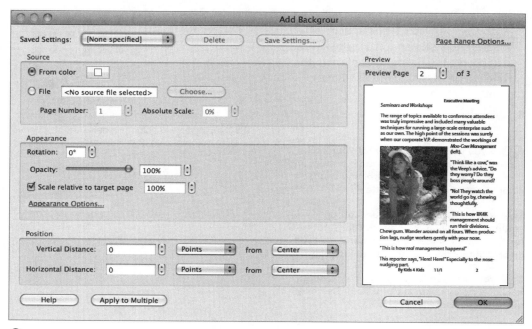

Ⓑ The Add Background dialog lets you apply a background color or artwork to your PDF pages.

3. Click the Browse (Windows) or Choose (Mac) button, and select the file that you want to use as the source of your background.

4. In the Page Number field, specify the page within the file you want to use.

5. In the Absolute Scale field, type the zoom percentage value you want to apply to the imported page.

    The preview reflects your choice of background 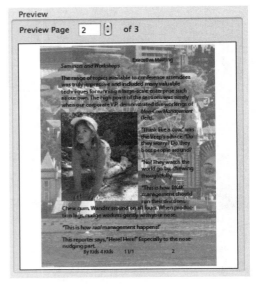 ⓒ.

6. Choose an opacity value for the background by using the slider control or typing a percentage into the text field.

    Reducing the opacity is important because it can keep the new background from overpowering the original page contents.

7. If you want your background to apply only to certain pages in your document, click the Page Range Options link (at the upper right in ⓑ) and specify which pages should be affected in the resulting dialog; the dialog is identical to the one we discussed in the header and footer section.

8. Click OK.

ⓒ The preview in the Add Background dialog reflects your currently chosen background.

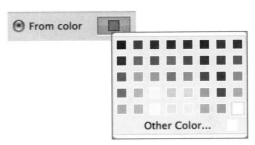

ⓓ To apply a solid color as a background, choose the color from the color-well control.

TIP If you want a solid color for your background, click the From Color radio button, and then click the color-well control and choose a color from the resulting palette ⓓ.

TIP You can save common background settings by clicking the Save Settings button. Acrobat lets you specify a name that will appear in the Saved Settings pop-up menu.

TIP You can modify or remove an existing background by choosing Update or Remove in the Background submenu ⓐ.

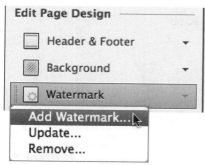

Edit Page Design

- Header & Footer
- Background
- Watermark
    - Add Watermark...
    - Update...
    - Remove...

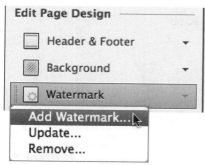

A You add, change, or remove a watermark by choosing the appropriate item from the Watermark submenu.

Adding a Watermark

A *watermark* is text or graphics that are placed on a page either in front of or behind the page's contents. The watermark can be text, a logo, or other page contents taken from another PDF, Illustrator, or image file.

To add a watermark to a document:

1. Choose Document > Watermark > Add Watermark **A**.

   Acrobat presents you with the Add Watermark dialog **B**.

2. If you want a text watermark, click the Text radio button.

continues on next page

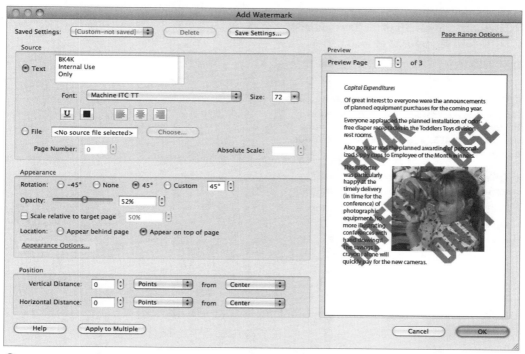

B The Add Watermark dialog lets you add text or artwork from another PDF file to your pages.

3. Type the text you want for your watermark.

4. Choose a font and size for the water-mark text.

5. Click one of the text-alignment buttons.

6. Choose an opacity value for the water-mark by using the Opacity slider or typing a percentage into the text field.

   It's important to reduce the watermark's opacity so that your original page contents remain readable.

7. Specify whether you want the water-mark in front of or behind the page contents by clicking the appropriate Location radio button.

8. If you want your watermark to apply to only certain pages in your document, click the Page Range Options link, as described in step 5 of the task "To add a header or footer to a document."

9. Click OK.

TIP **If you want to use a page in another PDF file as your watermark, click the File radio button and then follow the directions in the previous task, "To add a background to your document pages."**

TIP **You can modify or remove an existing watermark by choosing Update or Remove in the Watermark submenu Ⓐ.**

Adding Simple Navigation Features

If you intend for your PDF document to be read onscreen, you'll make life much easier for your reader if you provide some minimal tools for navigating the document. The easiest—and most consistently useful—navigation tools you can add to your document are bookmarks, links, and articles. These are the topics of this chapter.

Adding Bookmarks

Bookmarks constitute a clickable table of contents that resides in the Bookmarks navigation pane **Ⓐ**. Clicking a bookmark takes you to the corresponding view in the document.

A *view* in Acrobat is a combination of a page, a position on that page, and a zoom value **Ⓑ**.

To add a bookmark to a document, you set the document window to reflect the page, position, and zoom you want for that bookmark; then you create the bookmark, which records that view as its destination.

To create a bookmark in a document:

1. Using Acrobat's standard navigation tools, set the document window to display the view you want as the bookmark's target.

2. Open the Bookmarks navigation pane by clicking the Bookmark icon.

3. Click the New Bookmark icon at the top of the Bookmarks list **Ⓒ**.

   Acrobat inserts a new bookmark named Untitled into the Bookmarks pane. Untitled is already selected so you can type over it.

4. Type the name you want for the new bookmark.

5. Click outside the Bookmarks pane or press Enter (Return) to make the new name permanent.

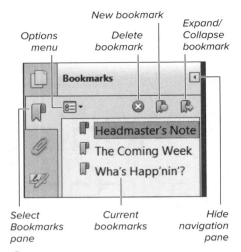

New bookmark
Options menu
Delete bookmark
Expand/ Collapse bookmark
Select Bookmarks pane
Current bookmarks
Hide navigation pane

Ⓐ Bookmarks make up a clickable table of contents that resides in the Bookmarks pane.

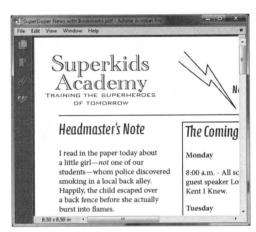

Ⓑ A bookmark's destination is a *view:* a combination of a page, a location on the page, and a zoom level.

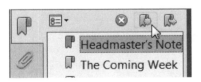

Ⓒ Clicking the New Bookmark icon creates a new bookmark named Untitled.

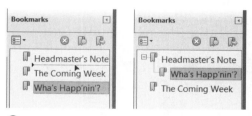

D If you select text and then create a new bookmark, the selected text becomes the bookmark's title.

E You can drag a bookmark to a new location in the Bookmarks list.

F The Bookmark Properties dialog lets you change the style and color of your bookmark's text in the Bookmarks list.

TIP Clicking a bookmark selects that bookmark in the list. When you create a new bookmark, it is inserted into the list immediately after the currently selected bookmark.

TIP If you select text on your document page with the Select tool **D** and then create a bookmark, the selected text becomes the new bookmark's name.

TIP You can easily rearrange bookmarks by dragging them to a new location in the list. A bit less obvious is the fact that you can drag a bookmark to be a descendent of another **E**. Once child bookmarks have been moved into another bookmark, you can display or hide them using the disclosure control to the left of the parent bookmark; this control is a plus sign in Windows and a triangle on the Macintosh, as usual.

TIP You can select and move multiple bookmarks at one time. To do so, hold down the Ctrl (Command) key to select individual bookmarks or the Shift key to select a contiguous range of bookmarks in the list.

TIP The top of the Bookmarks navigation pane also has buttons that let you delete a selected bookmark and go to the next bookmark (for when you're examining all of the destinations in the pane) **A**.

You can make a bookmark stand out in the list by changing its color or its text style.

To change a bookmark's color and text style:

1. Open the Bookmarks navigation pane, if necessary.

2. Right-click (Control-click) the bookmark whose properties you want to change.

3. Choose Properties.

   The Bookmark Properties dialog opens **F**.

continues on next page

4. Choose a text style from the drop-down menu.

   You can choose from the standard styles: bold, italic, and bold italic.

5. Click the color well, and choose a color from the resulting palette.

6. Click OK.

TIP **I often use a style to accentuate a document's structure. Bolding the bookmarks associated with chapter titles makes them stand out; in some documents, I'll make the bookmarks of the very important topics red.**

Sometimes you need to change the destination of a bookmark, often because you have changed the document—inserted new pages, perhaps—and the new contents are a better destination for the bookmark. Changing a bookmark's target is very easy to do.

To change a bookmark's destination:

1. Using Acrobat's standard navigation and zoom tools, set the document window so it displays the new destination you want for the bookmark.

2. Open the Bookmarks pane, if necessary.

3. Right-click (Control-click) the bookmark whose destination you want to change.

4. Choose Set Destination.

   Acrobat opens a dialog asking if you're sure you want to change the bookmark's destination 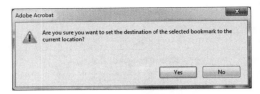.

5. Click Yes.

G When you change the destination of a bookmark, Acrobat gives you a chance to change your mind.

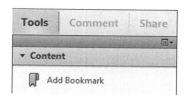

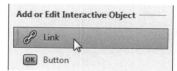

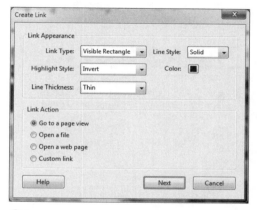

A The Link tool resides in the Content panel.

B The Create Link dialog lets you specify the appearance and behavior of a link.

The Acrobat User

The Acrobat User

The Acrobat User

The Acrobat User

C The highlight style specifies how a link changes when you click it. From top to bottom, they are None (boring), Invert, Outline, and Inset.

Creating Links

Links are the easiest way to make a PDF file a dynamic electronic document. They are, in effect, bookmarks that reside on your document page rather than in a navigation pane. They behave exactly like the links familiar to you on Web sites: You click the "hot" area of the link, and something happens—usually, the link sends you to another view in the document.

Links can have a visible border, but otherwise no icons or labels are associated with them. If you want such artwork, it must already be part of the contents of the PDF page. You lay the link on top of the existing graphics or text on the page.

You create links with the Link tool in the Content panel of the Tools pane **A**.

To create a link on a page:

1. In the Content panel, click the Link tool.

   The pointer changes to a crosshairs cursor.

2. Click and drag a rectangle on the PDF page where you want the link to be. Acrobat displays the Create Link dialog **B**.

3. Using the standard navigation and zoom tools, set the view in the document window to the destination of the new link.

4. If you want a visible rectangle around the link, choose Visible Rectangle in the Link Type drop-down menu; otherwise, choose Invisible Rectangle.

5. If you chose a visible rectangle for your link, specify the style, color, and thickness you want for the rectangle.

6. Choose a highlight style for the link **C**.

continues on next page

7. Among the Link Action radio buttons, click "Go to a page view." See the sidebar "Link Actions" for a discussion of the other actions.

8. Click Next.

   The Create Go to View dialog opens 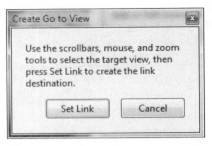. This dialog behaves like a palette, in that your Acrobat document is still active in the background; you can still use the navigation and zoom tools to move around in the document.

9. Use the navigation and zoom tools to set the document view to the link's destination.

10. Click the Set Link button.

    Acrobat returns your document window to the link's page. Your new link is visible as a bounding rectangle **E**; when you roll the pointer over this rectangle, handles appear at its sides and corners, as in the figure.

11. Adjust the position of the link by dragging its bounding rectangle.

12. Adjust the size of the link by dragging the handles at the sides and corners of its bounding rectangle.

13. To make another link, repeat steps 2–12.

14. When you're finished making links, click Acrobat's Hand tool or any other tool in the Tasks pane or toolbars.

D While the Create Go to View dialog is open, the document window is active in the background; you can use the arrow keys and other navigation tools to move around in the document.

The Acrobat User

E A link can be resized and repositioned by dragging the bounding rectangle or its handles with the Link tool.

Link Actions

The Create Link dialog **B** has four radio buttons you can choose from to specify what your link should do. The default action is "Go to a page view," which displays a new view in the document window when you click the link.

The other three radio buttons perform the following functions:

- **Open a file** creates a link that opens a spreadsheet, word-processing document, or other file on your computer, in whatever application is associated with that type of file. When you click the Next button in the Create Link dialog, Acrobat lets you specify the file to be opened.

- **Open a web page** tells the link to launch your default Web browser with a particular Web page. When you click the dialog's Next button, Acrobat opens a dialog in which you can type the URL of the Web page **F**.

F The Edit URL dialog lets you specify a Web address to associate with a link.

- **Custom link** provides access to more than a dozen advanced actions available to a link. Clicking Next takes you to the Actions tab in the Link Properties dialog **G**, whose Select Action menu lets you choose the action you want. This can be anything from playing a sound to executing an Acrobat menu item.

We'll talk about some of these actions in Chapter 13. However, most of them are beyond the scope of this book. See the Acrobat Help files for more information.

Interestingly, the advanced actions are also available to your bookmarks. If you right-click (Control-click) a bookmark and choose Properties, you get a dialog with the same Actions tab shown in **G**.

G The Actions tab in the Link Properties dialog lets you assign one of a variety of advanced actions to a link.

Modifying Existing Links

Whenever the Link tool is selected, all the links in your document appear as black bounding rectangles on the page. Clicking one of these rectangles selects that link; the bounding rectangle changes color, and handles appear whenever you move the pointer over the rectangle **Ⓐ**.

You can make a number of changes to a link when it's selected with the Link tool.

To modify an existing link:

1. Select the Link tool in the Content panel.

2. Click the link you want to modify.

3. To change the position of the link, drag its bounding rectangle to the new location.

4. Change the link's size by dragging the handles at its sides and corners.

5. To change the appearance of the link, right-click (Control-click) the link and choose Properties.

   Acrobat displays the Appearance controls in the Link Properties dialog, allowing you to reset the visibility, thickness, color, and other visual properties of the link **Ⓑ**.

6. To delete the link, press the Delete key.

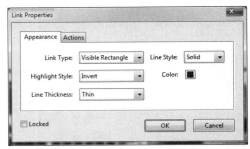

Ⓑ The Appearance controls in the Link Properties dialog give you the opportunity to adjust all the visual specifics of your link.

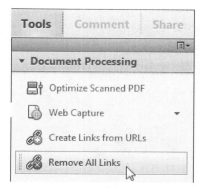

Ⓒ The Remove All Links tool removes all the links on particular pages in the document.

TIP You can change multiple links at one time. To do so, hold down the **Shift** or **Ctrl (Command)** key, and click the links you want to modify. Any changes you make apply to all the selected links.

TIP You can nudge the position and size of a selected link. Pressing an arrow key moves the selected link one pixel in the corresponding direction. Holding down the **Shift** key and pressing an arrow key moves the link 10 pixels. Finally, holding the Ctrl key (Option key on the Mac) while clicking arrow keys increases or decreases the size of the link by one pixel.

TIP You can delete all of the links in your document with a tool located in the Document Processing panel in the Tools pane Ⓒ. Just click the Remove All Links tool.

TIP You can also double-click a link with the Link tool to access the Link Properties dialog Ⓑ.

Making Automatic Web Links

The "Link Actions" sidebar discusses making a link to a Web page; when the reader clicks this link, Acrobat launches the default Web browser and opens the Web page tied to that link. Acrobat sensibly refers to such links as Web links.

Acrobat can automatically make Web links throughout your document. The Create Links from URLs tool is located in the Document Processing panel in the Tools pane **A**. When you click this tool, Acrobat searches the text in your PDF file and places links over any Web or email addresses it finds. Web addresses in the text receive links to that URL; email addresses get links that open the default mail client with a blank message addressed to the target email address.

To add Web links to your document:

1. With the document open to any page, select the Create Links from URLs tool in the Document Processing panel (in the Tools pane).

   Acrobat presents you with the Create Web Links dialog **B**.

2. Enter the beginning and ending page numbers of the range that should be scanned for URLs, or click All to select all pages.

3. Click OK.

   Acrobat scans your PDF file, adding links to all the URLs it finds. When it's finished, Acrobat reports on the number of links it added.

A The Create Links from URLs tool scans through your document, making links from any Web or email addresses it finds.

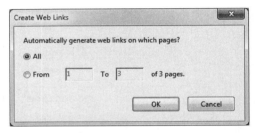

B The Create Web Links dialog lets you specify the pages that should be searched for URLs.

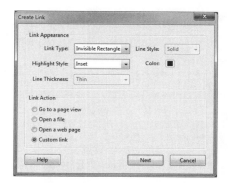

Creating a Next Page Button

Links make perfectly good navigation controls. However, they usually are associated with moving some distance within a document (a link to the index, for example) or to a different document entirely (such as to a Web site). For routine movement to the next or previous page, people generally expect a push button A.

In this section you'll add Next Page and Previous Page buttons to your document. The easiest way to do this is to make the button artwork part of the original page design, as in A, and then lay a link that does the work on top of each button.

The following task steps through the creation of a Next Page button. You can use nearly the same steps to create a Previous Page button.

These steps assume the button artwork is already on the page.

To create a Next Page button:

1. Click the Link tool on the Content panel.

2. Click and drag a link rectangle around the Next Page button's artwork.

   The Create Link dialog opens B.

3. Choose the following settings:

   ► For Link Type, choose Invisible Rectangle.

   ► For Highlight Style, choose Inset.

   ► For Link Action, choose Custom link.

4. Click Next.

   The Link Properties dialog opens C.

5. Click the Actions tab.

continues on next page

A We'll lay Next Page and Previous Page links on top of the button artwork already on the page.

B A Next Page button needs Custom link as its action.

C The Link Action for a Next Page button is "Execute a menu item."

6. In the Select Action pop-up menu, choose "Execute a menu item."

7. Click Add.

The Menu Item dialog opens 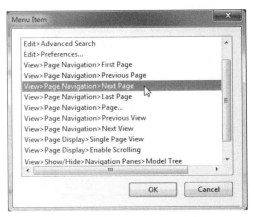. This dialog lists all the menu items in all of Acrobat's menus.

8. From the list choose View > Page Navigation > Next Page.

For a Previous Page button, you would choose View > Page Navigation > Previous Page.

9. Click OK.

Acrobat returns to the Link Properties dialog, which shows your chosen menu item in its list of Actions .

10. Click OK.

Acrobat returns you to your document page. The Next Page artwork is now surrounded by a link's blue border rectangle and handles .

11. Reposition and resize the link by dragging the rectangle and its handles.

12. Click the Hand tool (or any other tool) to indicate that you're finished creating the link.

When you click the Next Page button, Acrobat moves the document view to the next page.

TIP You can easily reproduce the Next Page link by copying it and then pasting it on other pages. Select the link with the Link tool, and then choose Edit > Copy (or use whatever technique you prefer to do a copy). Go to each page that has a Next Page button and paste the link onto the page.

TIP You can also add a Next Page button to your file as a Button object, but that is a much more involved process; we'll talk about that in Chapter 13.

D The menu item your link should execute is View > Page Navigation > Next Page.

E When you return to the Link Properties dialog, the menu item appears in the Actions list.

F With the Link tool still active, a rectangle surrounds the link that lets you position and resize the link so it fits the button artwork.

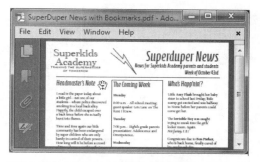

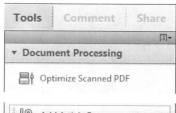

A When the pointer moves over an article, it becomes a hand with a down arrow.

B When you click an article (top), Acrobat zooms in until the article fills the width of the document window (bottom).

C The Add Article Box tool lets you create a series of linked boxes, together representing a single thread of text.

Creating Articles

An *article* in Acrobat is a set of rectangular regions scattered throughout your document that, taken together, represent a single thread of text. It's similar to an article in a newspaper, which may start on the front page, continue on pages 13 and 14, and finish up on page 27.

Articles are extremely useful for taking documents that were originally laid out for print—usually with a small point size, often with multiple columns—and making them readable online. I've used articles a lot in my documents and get embarrassingly enthusiastic about them!

When your pointer moves over an article on a page, the pointer turns into a hand with a down arrow **A**. When you click the article, Acrobat zooms in until the article exactly fits across the width of the document window **B**. This makes the text as easy to read as possible.

While you're reading an article, each click of the mouse button takes you down one screen in the article, changing from one column to another as needed. No scrolling, dragging, or fussing with navigation buttons is required.

When you reach the end of the article, a final click reverts the view to what it was before you entered the article.

To create an article in a document:

1. In the Document Processing panel, click the Add Article Box tool **C**.

   The pointer turns into a crosshair.

continues on next page

2. Click and drag a rectangle, indicating the first segment in the article .

3. Click and drag additional rectangles in the order that you want the reader to see them.

When you are finished, each of your article boxes is surrounded by a black rectangle labeled with an article number and a segment number **E**.

If you click a box with the Article tool, Acrobat provides you with the handles that allow you to resize the article.

4. When you've dragged out all the article segments, click the Article tool again (or any other tool) to indicate you're finished constructing your article.

Acrobat displays the Article Properties dialog **F**. The information this dialog requests is all optional, but it will make your article more useful to the reader.

5. Type in some combination of title, subject, author, and searchable keywords.

6. Click OK.

You've now created your article, which will behave properly as soon as you click the Hand tool.

TIP I sometimes use the Article tool to create a "linked list" of illustrations within my document. I create an article, each of whose boxes encloses one of the document's illustrations. In the final distributed document, the reader can click an illustration to enter the article and then click repeatedly to be taken from one illustration to the next.

Headmaster's Note

I read in the paper today about a little girl—*not* one of our students—whom police discovered smoking in a local back alley. Happily, the child escaped over a back fence before she actually burst into flames.

Time and time again our little community has been endangered by super children who are only barely in control of their powers.

D With the Article tool, you drag out a series of rectangles that will be the sections of your article text.

1-1
Headmaster's Note

I read in the paper today about a little girl—*not* one of our students—whom police discovered smoking in a local back alley. Happily, the child escaped over a back fence before she actually burst into flames.

Time and time again our little community has been endangered by super children who are only barely in control of their powers.

E Each section of your article is identified by an article number and a section number within that article. Each rectangle's handles let you resize the section.

Article Properties

Title: Headmaster's Note

Subject: Too-young superkids

Author: The Headmaster

Keywords:

OK   Cancel

F When you've defined all of the sections of your article, you can specify a title, subject, author, and searchable keywords for the article.

Setting Open Options

Having added your own navigation tools to your PDF document, you may want to hide Acrobat's native controls. This reduces visual clutter that would otherwise distract readers from your document's contents; ideally, they shouldn't have anything in front of their eyeballs except your information and message.

You control the presentation of your document by setting the file's "open options." These settings dictate how a document looks when it is opened. You can hide much of the Acrobat interface, specify what page should be initially displayed, and set several other characteristics that ensure your document is presented exactly as you wish.

Following are the steps that set the open options to what I consider the most useful settings in a document that provides its own navigation controls.

To set a document's open options:

1. Choose File > Properties.

   The Document Properties dialog opens 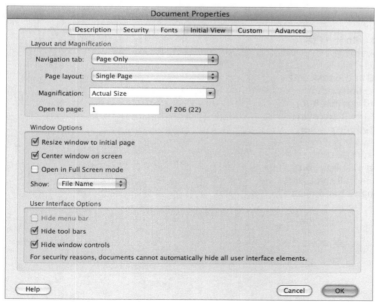.

2. Click the Initial View tab to see the controls that determine how the document will be presented to the user.

3. In the Navigation tab pop-up menu, choose Page Only.

   This option specifies that the Book-marks pane and other navigation panes be hidden.

4. In the Page layout pop-up menu, choose Single Page.

5. In the Magnification pop-up menu, choose Actual Size.

continues on next page

A The Initial View pane in the Document Properties dialog lets you specify what readers see when they first open your document.

6. Select the "Resize window to initial page" check box.

   The document opens in a window that exactly matches the page size. There won't be a gray border around the page in the document window.

7. Select the "Center window on screen" check box.

8. If you want your presentation to take over the entire screen, select the "Open in Full Screen mode" check box.

9. Select the "Hide tool bars" check box.

   This option hides the toolbars, which are an unnecessary distraction if you are supplying the document navigation.

10. Select the "Hide window controls" check box.

    This option hides the navigation pane icons, which are also unnecessary if you have your own Next Page buttons.

Steps 9 and 10 result in your document window displaying only page content, with no buttons or other controls .

TIP Open options are stored with the PDF file, so they travel with the document.

TIP Full Screen mode (step 8 in the task list) is useful for corporate presentations or for kiosk documents. I recommend against it for other situations; most people find it annoying when a document covers everything else on their computers.

TIP The Open Options dialog also lets you hide the Acrobat menu bar. Generally, you shouldn't do this; hiding the menu bar makes most readers uncomfortable.

B You can minimize the distractions in an Acrobat presentation by hiding the toolbars and other user interface elements.

Adding Multimedia To Your File

Up to now, we have been discussing documents that are, at root, replacements for printed documents; the pages we have worked with conceptually consist of marks on paper: text, line art, and images that can be reproduced on a printer.

However, in this modern, twenty-first century world of ours, documents are no longer static collections of ink marks. We increasingly expect that a document should include sound and video when appropriate.

Acrobat accommodates multimedia content perfectly well. In this chapter, you'll learn how to embed movies, sounds, and Flash animation in your PDF documents.

In This Chapter

Placing a Movie on a Page

Acrobat lets you import Flash multimedia files and movies that are H.264 compliant. (H.264 is a video standard that is compact and high quality, and can be implemented by a broad range of movie types, including MOV and MP4.)

The embedded movies can be played by Adobe Acrobat 9 or Reader 9 and later.

Acrobat plays these movie files on its own, without requiring external applications, such as QuickTime Player or Windows Movie Player. As a result, the animation is guaranteed to have a consistent appearance on all platforms. You also automatically get some very nice-looking navigation controls that the reader can use to control the video.

However, these animations will play only with Acrobat 9 or later; older versions of Acrobat will not be able to play them. (You'll get a warning immediately upon trying to open the file with an earlier version of Acrobat.) Also, because the movies are stored internally as Flash-based animations, they won't play on devices that don't support Flash; the Apple iPhone and iPad come immediately to mind.

You place movies on a PDF page using the Multimedia menu in the Content panel of the Tools pane .

> **TIP** If your placed movies need to be compatible with Acrobat 8 or earlier, you will need to dust off your copy of Acrobat 9; that version of Acrobat could import "legacy" format movies, which are playable in Acrobat 6 or later.

A The Multimedia controls reside in a menu toward the bottom of the Content panel.

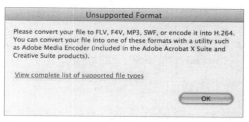

B The Insert Video dialog lets you specify the movie you want to place on the page.

C Acrobat warns you if the movie you pick isn't a Flash animation or H264-compliant movie.

D The placed movie appears on the page as a "poster" with a small Play button in its lower-left corner.

E Moving the pointer over a playing movie reveals a set of controls for pausing, scrolling, and otherwise controlling the movie's playback.

To place a movie on a PDF page:

1. Choose Multimedia > Video in the Content panel of the Tools pane **A**.

   The pointer turns into a crosshair.

2. Click and drag a rectangle on the page where you want to place the movie. (This rectangle will be resized to match the movie's dimensions, so don't worry about precision here.)

   Acrobat presents you with the Insert Video dialog **B**.

3. Click Choose and select the movie file in the resulting pick-a-file dialog.

   This file must be either a Flash animation document or an H.264-compatible movie file. If it is not, Acrobat tells you that it can't import the movie and reminds you of the types of movie files it *can* import **C**.

4. Click OK.

   Acrobat places the movie on the page. The placed movie appears as a poster (usually the first frame in the movie; see the following task) with a Play button superimposed in its lower-left corner **D**. (This looks like a button, but it isn't. It's simply an icon that labels this item as a movie.)

To play the movie, simply click anywhere in the movie's image on the page.

Whenever the mouse pointer is over the movie while it's playing, a set of translucent controls appears over the movie, allowing the user to pause, rewind, and otherwise control the movie **E**.

continues on next page

TIP Movies placed within a document are embedded in the PDF file; this means that the PDF file size will increase by the size of the movies it contains. This can result in *very* large PDF files.

TIP Acrobat X internally converts all movies to Flash animations; this is why they require Acrobat 9 or later to play.

Each movie you have placed in your file has a *poster,* a picture that is displayed on the page when the movie isn't playing. The default poster is the first frame of the movie, which is acceptable much of the time. You can easily customize this, however, using any picture file on your disk as the movie's poster.

To customize a movie's poster:

1. In the Content panel, choose Multimedia > Video, and then double-click on a placed movie.

   Acrobat displays the Edit Video dialog **F**.

2. Click the "Create poster from file" radio button.

3. Click Choose and select an image file in the resulting pick-a-file dialog.

4. Click OK.

TIP The Edit Video dialog has several controls that affect how your movie is controlled and played. The default settings for these controls are all reasonable, but you should look them over when you have a moment to get an idea of the possibilities available to you.

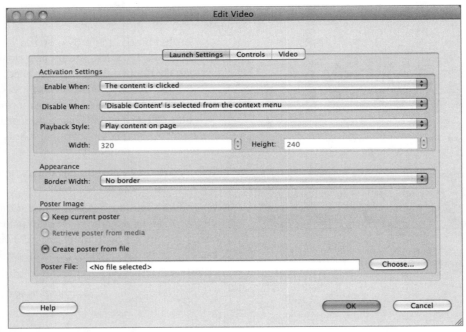

F The Edit Video dialog has a large collection of controls that affect the characteristics of your movie.

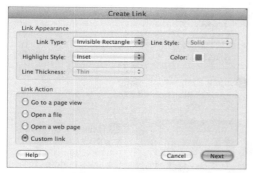

Creating Movie Controls

Once a movie has been placed, you can play it by clicking it with the Hand tool. However, you may want to provide your own controls for playing, pausing, and quitting the movies. This is easily done with links.

The easiest way to create a Play Movie button is to place the button artwork on the page in the original document design **A**. You can then lay links on top of the button graphic to do the actual work.

The following task steps through the creation of a Play button. Making buttons for Stop, Pause, and other commands is done virtually the same way. The steps presume the Play button's artwork is already on the PDF page.

A To create movie controls, start with the button artwork already placed on the page.

B We'll create an Acrobat link with a "Custom link" action.

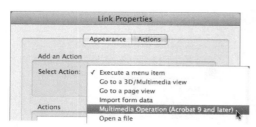

C In the Link Properties dialog, specify that the link should perform a multimedia operation.

To create a Play button:

1. Click the Link tool on the Content panel.

2. Click and drag a link rectangle around the Play button's artwork.

   The Create Link dialog opens **B**.

3. Choose the following settings:

   ▸ For Link Type, choose Invisible Rectangle.

   ▸ For Highlight Style, choose Inset.

   ▸ For Link Action, choose Custom link.

4. Click Next.

   The Link Properties dialog opens **C**. (You saw this dialog in Chapter 12.)

5. Click the Actions tab.

6. In the Select Action pop-up menu in the Link Properties dialog, choose Multimedia Operation (Acrobat 9 and later) **C**.

continues on next page

7. Click Add.

Acrobat presents you with the Multi-media Operations dialog . This dialog will display all of the movies placed in the file.

8. Select the movie that you want the link to control.

9. In the Action menu, choose Play.

This is where you would make a Pause or Stop button. The pop-up menu has all the actions you might perform with a movie: Pause, Rewind, and so on 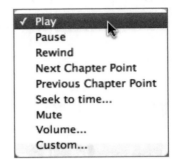.

10. Click OK.

Acrobat returns you to the Link Properties dialog, which now shows Multimedia Operation in its Actions list.

11. Click OK.

Acrobat returns you to your page, which now has a link rectangle with handles that you can use to reposition and resize the link as needed .

12. Click the Hand tool in the Quick Tools toolbar to finalize the link.

When you click your new Play button, Acrobat plays the movie.

D The Multimedia Operations dialog lets you specify which movie the link should control.

E A link can perform many useful operations on a movie.

F Having placed your link over the button artwork, you can use the link's handles to get the fit just right.

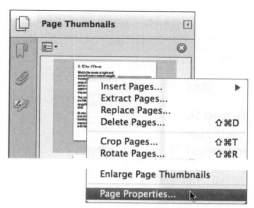

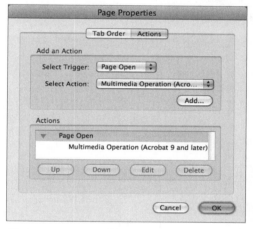

G The first step in having a movie or sound automatically play when a page opens is to access the Page Properties from the Page Thumbnails navigation pane.

H Choose the Page Open action from the Tab Order pane of the Page Properties dialog.

Automatic movies

In some cases, you might want the movie to automatically play when the reader opens its page. You do this by creating a page action that Acrobat carries out when the reader enters a particular page. Your page action will play a movie.

To automatically play a movie when a page opens:

1. With your document open, display the Page Thumbnails navigation pane by clicking its icon at the right side of the page.

2. Right-click (Control-click) the thumbnail of the page that has your movie **G**.

3. Choose Page Properties.

   The Page Properties dialog opens **H**.

4. Click the Actions tab.

5. In the Select Trigger pop-up menu, choose Page Open.

   This option tells Acrobat to play the movie when the reader opens the page rather than when the reader closes it.

6. Follow steps 6–12 in the previous task, "To create a Play button," assigning a Multimedia Operation to the page action.

   Acrobat will now play the movie every time the page is opened.

Placing a Flash Animation on the Page

In the previous section of this chapter, we added Flash files, often suffixed .swf, to a page as embedded movies. You can also place a SWF file on the page as a Flash animation. The advantage of doing this is that all of the interactive parts within the Flash animation—links, buttons, sliders, and the like—are active; if the Flash file has a slider that controls the speed of the animation, that slider works exactly as it should.

You can place any kind of SWF file on the PDF page: games, counters, and so on—anything bundled as a SWF file. They will all behave properly, and all the pieces will work.

You get a whole lot of bang for your nickel when you import Flash files this way.

The following instructions are brief because importing a SWF file follows the same path as importing a movie, and the dialogs and controls are virtually identical to those in our previous discussion.

Ⓐ Importing a SWF file places the file on the PDF page with all of its interactive parts intact.

To place a Flash animation on the page:

1. Choose Multimedia > SWF in the Content panel Ⓐ.

   The pointer turns into a crosshair.

2. Click and drag a rectangle on the page where you want the movie to be placed.

   Acrobat presents you with the Insert SWF dialog 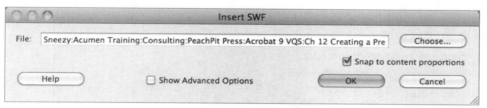 ⑧.

3. Click the Choose button and select the SWF file in the resulting pick-a-file dialog.

4. Click OK.

   Acrobat places the Flash animation on the page. Users can play the Flash animation by clicking it. Curiously, once started, an animation can be stopped again only by right-clicking (Control-clicking) it and choosing (not very obviously) Disable Content ⓒ.

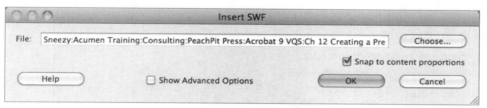

⑧ The Insert SWF dialog is nearly identical in appearance and behavior to the Insert Video dialog.

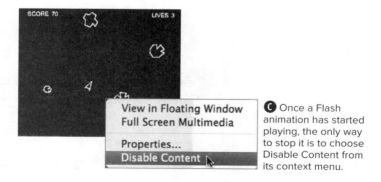

ⓒ Once a Flash animation has started playing, the only way to stop it is to choose Disable Content from its context menu.

Adding Sound
to a PDF Page

Acrobat lets you attach an MP3 sound to a page in your PDF file. This sound could be part of your document's content ("Click here for a personal message from our candidate") or background music for your presentation. Acrobat plays these sounds directly without using an external utility (such as QuickTime Player or Windows Movie Player); this ensures that the sound will play correctly on all systems.

Embedding a sound on a PDF page is identical to embedding a movie except you start with the Sound tool rather than the Movie tool.

To place a sound on a document page:

1. In the Content panel of the Tools pane, choose Multimedia > Sound.

2. Click and drag a rectangle on the page.

   The Insert Sound dialog opens 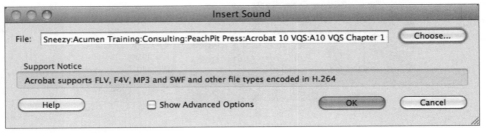.

3. Click the Choose button and select the sound file in the pick-a-file dialog.

4. Click OK.

Ⓐ The Insert Sound dialog is identical to the Insert Video dialog and is used exactly the same way.

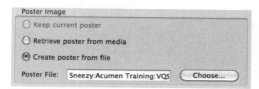

B A sound file placed on the page will display a set of tiny controls so you can pause, stop, and restart the sound.

Poster Image

○ Keep current poster

○ Retrieve poster from media

◉ Create poster from file

Poster File: | Sneezy:Acumen Training:VQS | Choose...

C The Advanced Options section of the Insert Sound dialog lets you create a poster for the sound; this will represent the sound on the PDF page.

When you're finished, your sound will appear as a rectangle with a little Play button in it, exactly as you saw when embedding a movie except the rectangle is empty (sounds don't have a poster frame). When you click the rectangle, Acrobat plays the sound and displays some (sometimes very tiny) controls that let you pause, adjust the volume, and so on **B**.

TIP Although sounds don't automatically get a poster applied to them, you can provide a picture to use as a marker on the page. In the Add Sound dialog, click the Advanced Options button, choose "Create poster from File," and select a TIFF, JPEG, or other picture file to use as a poster **C**.

TIP As with videos, you can have Acrobat automatically play a sound (a bugle fanfare, perhaps) when the user opens the page. Follow the directions for attaching a movie to a page (see "Placing a Movie on a Page" earlier in this chapter), but choose a sound file instead of a movie file.

TIP Use automatic sounds with restraint. A sound that plays every time a reader passes through a page can get really annoying after a few hundred repetitions.

Creating Forms
with Acrobat Pro

Acrobat Pro has long provided tools that let you define interactive form fields that can collect data from a reader and send that data back to you.

At this point in its evolution, the Acrobat form mechanism is very rich and is worthy of a book or two on its own. This chapter introduces you to the basics of creating a functioning form with Acrobat. Fortunately, you can get very far with just the basics. And Adobe has rethought and rearranged how the form features in Acrobat X work, making it much easier to find the tools you need while you are designing your form.

Once your form is created, Acrobat X's integration with Acrobat.com makes it mindlessly simple to distribute it to numerous people and retrieve their responses. Acrobat X handles all the details of posting your form online, sending out notices to your list of responders and then collecting the information they provide.

Creating and distributing Acrobat forms has never been easier.

In This Chapter

Creating a Form

All the tools you use to work with forms—for creating, distributing, and collecting—are accessible through the aptly named Forms panel in the Tools pane .

Acrobat's forms tools assume that you are starting with an existing electronic or paper document that you need to convert to an active PDF form. This is an excellent assumption; many corporations today find themselves with a collection of paper forms they want to convert to PDF forms that can be filled out electronically.

Acrobat X has made this a relatively straightforward task; the only prerequisite is that the form must be in an electronic format. It can be a scanned paper form, a document designed with Illustrator and exported to PDF, or any file type that Acrobat knows how to convert to PDF.

This file will look like a form, but there are no active form fields on the page; the fill-in-the-blank lines are just graphic lines, the check boxes only squares .

Converting the electronic file to a PDF interactive form is easy. Acrobat X will convert the form to PDF, if necessary, and then apply its Form Field Recognition feature, which analyzes the file and automatically places appropriate form fields on the new PDF page. Although Form Field Recognition gives you an excellent start, you'll probably need to add some additional form fields manually, using the Forms panel . Acrobat often fails to recognize some of the fill-in spaces in the original document. You'll learn how to do this later.

Still, Acrobat does an amazingly good job for a first pass; you're left, relatively speaking, with just cleanup.

A The tools you use to work with interactive forms all live in the Forms panel in the Tools pane.

B When you convert an electronic document to a form, your starting document looks like a form but isn't one. The lines and squares are just lines and squares, not form fields.

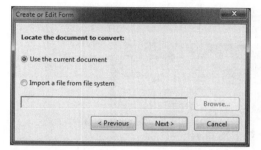

C To convert a PDF file or scanned paper form to an Acrobat form, select "Use the current document or browse to a file."

D The Create or Edit Form wizard asks you to pick the document you want to convert. Or you can use the currently open PDF file.

To convert an electronic file into a form:

1. In the Forms panel of the Tools pane, click Create **A**.

   The Create or Edit Form Wizard opens **C**.

2. Choose "Use the current document or browse to a file" and click Next.

   Acrobat presents you with the second pane in the Wizard, which asks you to locate the document you want to convert **D**.

3. Do one of the following:
   - ▸ If the document is already open in the current window, select "Use the current document."
   - ▸ Otherwise, select "Import a file from file system," click the Browse button, and then select the PDF or image file you want to convert.

4. Click the Next button.

   Acrobat displays a progress bar and spends some time converting and importing the document. Although this process is usually fast, it can sometimes take a remarkably long time, so don't cancel the process until a few minutes have elapsed.

   continues on next page

When Acrobat is finished processing the file, it presents you with a new form in the Form Editor ⓔ. The PDF pages will have many form fields already in place, which were put there by the Form Field Recognition feature; clicking any of these fields presents you with a rectangular border with the usual handles ⓕ.

5. Resize and reposition the existing form fields so that they fit the page's artwork appropriately.

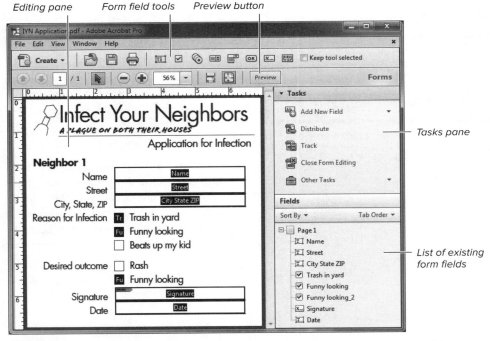

ⓔ After Acrobat has converted your file, it sends you to the Form Editor, where you can add new form fields and tweak existing ones.

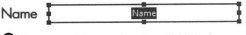

ⓕ When you click one of the form fields in the Form Editor, the bounding rectangle displays handles you can use to resize the field.

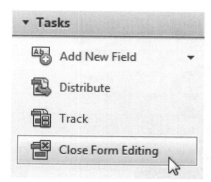

G When you are finished adding fields to your form, click the Close Form Editing button.

H When you return to the Acrobat Hand tool, your form fields are in place and functioning on the page. Note the new toolbar with instructions and a Highlight Existing Fields button.

6. Click Close Form Editing in the Tasks pane **G**.

Acrobat closes the Form Editor and returns you to the document window, displaying the newly placed form fields **H**.

Note that the finished form sports a new toolbar at the top and has all the form fields highlighted in a light blue. The user can turn off the highlighting by clicking the Highlight Existing Fields button in the toolbar.

Acrobat will probably have missed some of the form fields you need on the page; for example, in **H**, Acrobat did not place two of the check boxes, so you'll need to add those fields by hand.

TIP In step 2, you could also have selected "Scan a paper form," in which case Acrobat will send you to its scanner interface (which was discussed in Chapter 4); the scanned document is then opened in the Form Editor, complete with initial form fields.

To add form fields to a form:

1. In the document window's Form panel, click Edit.

   Acrobat opens the Form Editor **E**.

2. Click the Add New Field button (in the Form Editor's Tasks pane) to access a drop-down list of available form fields **I**. Select the type of field you want to add to the page.

   The pointer turns into a peculiar-looking ghost rectangle with a dotted-line crosshair **J**.

3. You can either click once on the PDF page, which places a form field on the page the same size as the "ghost," or drag out a rectangle, which gives you a new form field the size of the rectangle you dragged. Either way, you get a form field on the page with a yellow floating palette immediately adjacent to it **K**.

4. Type a name in the palette's Field Name field.

   This is an internal name and is not visible on the final form page; it can be any arbitrary string of characters, although I recommend something appropriate to the field's purpose.

5. If this field represents required data—that is, data that the user must supply before closing the form, such as name or zip code—select the "Required field" check box.

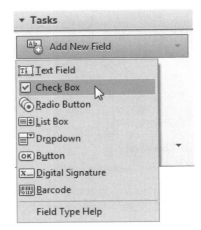

I To place a new form field on the page, select the appropriate form field type from the Add New Field menu in the Form Editor's Tasks pane.

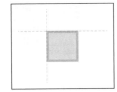

J When placing a new form field, the pointer turns into a "ghost" of the form field with a dotted-line crosshair extending beyond it.

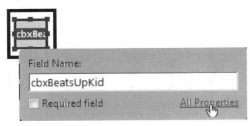

K When you place your form field, it appears as a rectangle with handles and an adjacent palette into which you can type a name for the field.

6. Reposition and resize the new field so it matches the page's artwork.

   You can nudge the position of the field with your arrow keys and nudge the size with Control-arrow keys.

7. Repeat steps 2 through 6 for each form field you need to add to the page.

8. When all is to your liking, click the Close Form Editing button in the Tasks pane ⓖ.

TIP The Form Editor provides a series of buttons, one for each type of form field, in its toolbar ⓛ. I find these useful when I'm making several new form fields. It's more convenient just to click the Text Field button, for example, rather than choosing Text Field from the Add New Field menu.

TIP At any time while you are working in the Form Editor, you can see exactly how the form will look to the user by clicking the Preview button in the Favorites toolbar ⓛ.

TIP If you are partway through creating a form and have to put it aside (there are only so many hours in a day), you can resume adding fields by opening the file in Acrobat and selecting Edit in the Forms panel. Acrobat returns you to the Form Editor.

TIP If you click the All Properties link visible in ⓚ, Acrobat displays a Field Properties dialog specific to the type of field you just created ⓜ. Most of the controls here have reasonable defaults, but I suggest you take a look at them in your idle moments. You can access the same dialog by right-clicking (Control-clicking) a field in the Form Editor and choosing Properties.

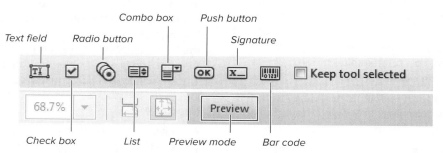

Text field   Radio button   Combo box   Push button   Signature

Check box   List   Preview mode   Bar code

ⓛ The Form Editor's toolbar provides a handy button for each field type. Just click one of these buttons to add a new field to the page.

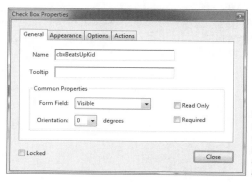

ⓜ The Field Properties dialog (here shown for a check box) lets you specify the appearance and other properties of a form field.

Distributing Forms

In times past, one of the most trouble-some parts of using Acrobat for your forms was distributing them and then some-how getting information back from your respondents. With Acrobat X, distributing your form to a group of respondents is satisfyingly simple. Acrobat does all the bookkeeping necessary to send the form to your readers and collect the responses from them.

Acrobat lets you distribute your form in three ways:

- **Acrobat.com.** This is the preferred way of distributing forms. Acrobat uploads your form to Acrobat.com and then emails a file link to your recipients. They click the emailed link, fill out the form, and then click the Submit Form button in the document window. Their responses are uploaded to Acrobat. com. You can examine the responses any time in Acrobat.

  Your form recipients must use Acrobat 9 or Adobe Reader 9 or later to fill in and return the form.

- **Your own server.** This is the same as distributing a form by Acrobat.com except that you use your own server to store the form and its responses. We won't be discussing this option in this book; Acrobat.com is free and easy, and is a much better way to distribute forms.

- **Email.** This is how you distribute forms if your recipients include people with very old versions of Acrobat (and no amount of batting about the head will get them to upgrade).

  Acrobat sends the form to your list of recipients attached to an email message. The recipients open the attachment, fill out the form, and click a Submit Form button in the document window; then the completed form is automatically emailed back to you. You can open the returned form and examine the responses.

  Your form recipients must use Acrobat 6 or Adobe Reader 6 or later to fill in and return the form.

Note that in all cases Acrobat tracks your form's progress. To whom has the form been sent? Who has responded? What information did the recipient type into the form fields? All of this is handled by Acrobat and is accessible through the Tracker window, which you last saw when we discussed document reviews in Chapter 9.

As one who has worked with people for years setting up form distribution and response workflows, let me assure you that this is way cool.

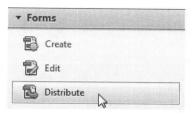

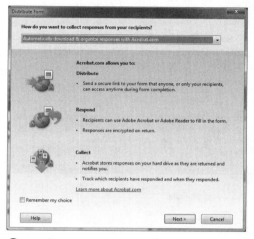

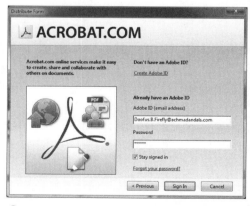

(A) The first step in distributing a form to a group of people is to click the Distribute tool in the Forms panel.

(B) When you choose Distribute in the Forms panel, Acrobat presents you with a dialog that lets you specify how to distribute your form. We'll use Acrobat.com.

(C) You are asked to sign in to Acrobat.com.

Distributing a form with Acrobat.com

The most efficient way to distribute a form is by using Acrobat.com. In this case, your form and all the bookkeeping information associated with it (including the responses from your recipients) are stored on Acrobat.com. The advantage is that you don't need to receive each responder's information one at a time; you can simply open the Tracker periodically to get the currently submitted responses.

In addition, all the recipients' responses are compiled into a single file rather than being scattered among a series of individual PDF files.

To distribute a form with Acrobat.com:

1. With the form open in Acrobat, click the Distribute tool in the Forms panel of the Tools pane **(A)**.

    The Distribute Form Wizard opens **(B)**.

2. In the drop-down menu, choose "Automatically download & organize responses with Acrobat.com," and then click the Next button. Acrobat displays the next panel in the Distribute Form Wizard, which asks you to sign in to Acrobat.com **(C)**. You can also create a new Acrobat.com account, if necessary.

    continues on next page

3. Sign in to Acrobat.com, and then click the SIgn In button.

Acrobat spends a few seconds talking to the Acrobat.com server and then displays the next panel in the Distribute Form Wizard **D**.

4. In the To field, enter the email addresses, separated by commas, of all the people you want notified of the form's availability.

Note that this panel of the Wizard has a drop-down menu that lets you specify who should have access to this form: anyone who knows the URL or only the people you notified by email **E**.

Also note that you can alter the subject and message body.

5. Click Send.

Acrobat uploads your file to Acrobat.com, sends your email notifications, and then opens the Tracker window so you can see the status of your newly posted form **F**.

Your form is now available to your chosen responders.

TIP In step 4, you can click the To button and take addresses from your system's address book.

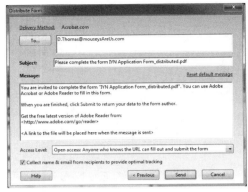

D You supply the email addresses of the people you want notified of your form's availability.

E You can specify that your form may be viewed by anyone who knows your form's URL or only by people to whom you sent notices.

F You can later see your recipients' replies through the Forms Tracker.

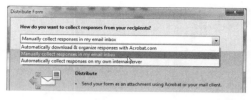

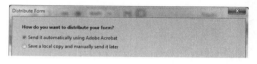

G When you choose Distribute in the Forms panel, Acrobat presents you with a dialog that lets you specify how to distribute your form. We'll send our form by email.

H Acrobat asks whether it should email your form to your recipients or whether you want to do it.

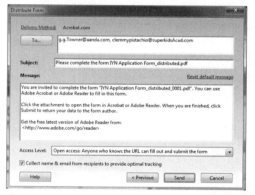

I Finally, you supply the email addresses of the people to whom the form should be sent. You can also edit the subject and message body.

Distributing forms by email

The only problem with using Acrobat.com to distribute your forms (and it is the *only* problem) is that it requires the recipients to have at least Acrobat or Reader 9 to fill in and return the form. If you have clients who persist in using older versions of Acrobat, you should distribute your form as an attachment to an email message.

As with the server-based distribution, you can do this directly from within Acrobat, letting the software keep track of responses.

To distribute a form by email:

1. With the form open in Acrobat, click the Distribute tool in the Forms panel.

   The Distribute Form Wizard opens as before **G**. This dialog lets you choose how to distribute the form.

2. In the drop-down menu, choose "Manually collect responses in my email inbox" and then click the Next button.

   Acrobat displays the second panel in the Distribute Form Wizard, which asks if you want Acrobat to email the form to your recipients or if you want to do it yourself **H**. Here, we'll have Acrobat do the mailing.

3. Select "Send it automatically using Adobe Acrobat" and click Next.

   Acrobat displays the final step of the Distribute Form Wizard, asking you for the email addresses of the form's recipients **I**.

continues on next page

4. Type in the To field the email addresses of all the people to whom the form should be sent.

The addresses can be on separate lines within the field or separated by semicolons.

You can also edit the email's subject and message text.

5. Click Send.

Acrobat sends your form as an attachment to the email addresses you provided. Depending on your system and email client, Acrobat may send the email directly or it may open your mail client with an appropriate message open, ready for you to click Send.

When recipients receive the form and open it in Acrobat, they see an instruction panel at the top of the document window . This panel contains instructions on what to do with the form and a Submit Form button. It also contains a button that lets the user highlight the form fields in light blue so that they are easy to see.

The recipient fills out the form and then clicks the Submit Form button. Acrobat uses the recipient's mail client to send the completed form back to you.

J Whoever receives your form sees a brief set of instructions and two buttons at the top of the form's page.

A Your recipients receive an email that contains a link to the form on Acrobat.com.

B As a recipient of a form, clicking the emailed link takes you to Acrobat.com, which asks if you want to download the form file or open it in your Web browser. I usually download it to my disk, but both options work well.

Responding to a Distributed Form

If you are one of the recipients of a form distributed by Acrobat X, you will receive an emailed notice inviting you to review the document **A**.

Depending on how the form was distributed, the email message will either have the form file as an attachment or contain a link to the form file's location on Acrobat.com.

To respond to a distributed form:

1. Open the form in Acrobat X or Adobe Reader X; you do this one of two ways:

   ▸ If the form file is attached to the email message, simply open the file in Acrobat X as you would any other attachment.

   ▸ If the email contains a link, click that link; your Web browser opens and takes you to Acrobat.com, which presents you with a button that automatically downloads and opens the file **B**. Click this Download button and then open the form.

continues on next page

You are now looking at the PDF form whose document window has the instructions and buttons we described in the previous section **C**.

2. Fill out the form.

3. Click the Submit Form button.

   Acrobat acts according to how the form was distributed: It will either use your email client to email the completed form back to the sender or upload your form data to Acrobat.com.

TIP The form fields in the document are initially shaded a blue tint to make them obvious. You can toggle this blue shading by clicking the Highlight Existing Fields button at the top of the form's window.

C The form's window displays some instructional text and two buttons at the top.

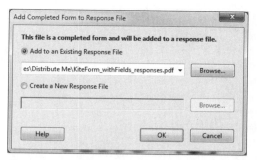

Receiving and Viewing Results

Acrobat X makes it remarkably easy to receive and view responses to your form. The secret is the Tracker, which takes care of all the grunt work entailed in managing form data returned by your recipients.

Furthermore, the Tracker handles *all* your forms, whether you sent them by email or you distributed them through Acrobat.com.

Receiving emailed form responses

Before you can view responses to your form, you must collect them from Acrobat.com or the respondents' emails. Collecting responses from Acrobat.com happens automatically; you don't need to explicitly import them.

For forms that you distributed by email, you must open the returned form (attached to the emailed response) and tell Acrobat to add that file's form data to the collection of responses. It's much easier than it sounds.

To receive emailed form responses:

1. In your email software, open the email with the attached, completed form.

2. Open the attached PDF file.

   In most systems, you can do this directly from the email client.

   A dialog opens notifying you that the form belongs to an ongoing form distribution and asking permission to add the data to that form's collection of responses **A**. Note that you will see references to a "response file" in this and other form-related dialogs; this is a file in which Acrobat keeps bookkeeping information about a distributed form.

continues on next page

3. Click OK.

Acrobat adds the form's responses to the collection and then opens the Tracker so you can examine the results.

Viewing form responses

The Tracker is Grand Central Station for viewing the responses to all of your distributed forms. You access the Tracker by clicking Track in the Forms panel **B**. The resulting Tracker window gives you access to all the forms you have distributed, whether by email or by Acrobat.com **C**.

The left side of this window displays a hierarchical list of all the forms you have in distribution **D**. When you click one of the forms in the list, the right side of the window fills with information and a collection of links leading to more information about that form, including a list of who has and who has not responded to the form.

This is the same Tracker used in Chapter 9 to examine responses to document reviews.

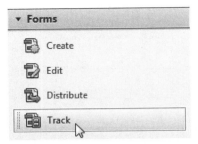

B To launch the Forms Tracker, you click the Track tool in the Forms panel.

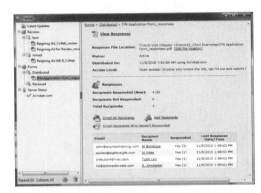

C The Forms Tracker is the tool you use to manage the replies to your form.

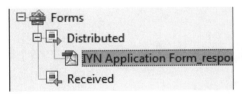

D The Tracker window has a list of all your currently distributed forms. Select one of these to examine its responses.

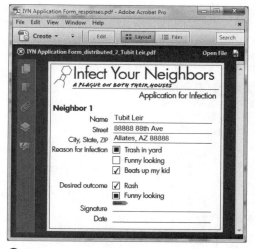

E Clicking the Tracker's View Responses link yields an Acrobat portfolio that lists all the replies received so far.

F Double-clicking a reply in the Responses portfolio displays the form page with the recipient's responses in place.

G You return to the list of responses by clicking the close link in the upper-left corner of the response window.

H The Responses portfolio has a collection of controls that let you carry out a variety of tasks.

To view the responses for all returned forms:

1. Click Track in the Forms panel of the Tools pane.

   The Tracker window opens **C**.

2. In the left side of the window, select the distributed form whose responses you want to examine.

   The right side displays that form's respondents.

3. Click the View Responses link in the right side of the window, at the top.

   Acrobat creates a portfolio that lists all the responses received for this form and provides tools for examining, archiving, and otherwise working with those responses **E**.

4. Double-click one of the responses in the list.

   Acrobat displays that filled-in form **F**. Look it over; think hard on the implications of the response given in each form field.

5. Click the close link at the top of the document window to return to the list of response files **G**.

TIP The Responses portfolio has a set of command buttons **H** that provide several functions, such as filtering responses and exporting them to a file.

TIP The Responses portfolio's Update button (at the top of its column of buttons **H**) is particularly useful for forms distributed by Acrobat.com. It checks to see if there have been any additional responses posted and adds them to the list, if so.

LiveCycle Designer

The Windows version of Acrobat X Pro ships with a copy of a stand-alone form creation tool named LiveCycle Designer 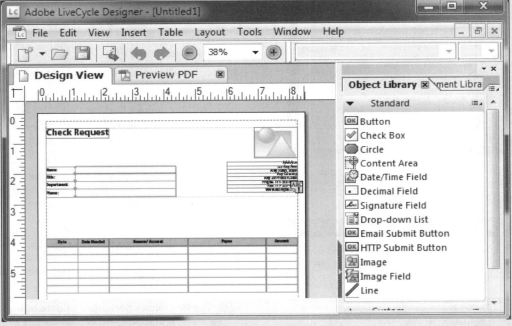. This program, which you'll find in your Start menu, offers an alternative to creating forms directly in Acrobat. Its most important feature is a large collection of templates that let you create a PDF form from scratch rather than needing an existing file with artwork already placed on the page.

Creating a form with LiveCycle Designer has much of the flavor of using a simple graphics package. If you know how to use this chapter's form tools, you'll pick up LiveCycle Designer in no time.

You will probably find, however, that if you are adding form fields to an existing file, as described in this chapter, the Acrobat form tools are more efficient.

As a historical note, Acrobat 8 and 9 integrated LiveCycle Designer into the Acrobat forms mechanism; Acrobat X splits it out into a separate, much less visible tool.

I LiveCycle Designer is a stand-alone form creation tool that ships with the Windows version of Acrobat X.

Protecting Your Document

An increasing proportion of the world's documents are distributed as PDF files, many of which are to a greater or lesser extent confidential. Banks don't want their customers' financial statements read by just anyone; software companies need to keep new product specifications from the eyes of their competitors; and most of us don't want our love letters broadcast for the world to read.

Acrobat offers three levels of security to control access to a PDF file:

- **Password security.** A password is required to open the PDF file.

- **Password restriction.** A password is required to print, modify, or otherwise work with the file.

- **Redaction.** Parts of the file contents are permanently "blacked out," preventing them from being read. There is no password; the redacted text and images are simply unavailable to the reader.

You can also restrict access to the file based on a digital signature, but we'll talk about that in the next chapter.

Restricting File Access

The most effective protection you can apply to a file is to password-protect access to it; viewers are not allowed to see the file's contents unless they know the Magic Word. The file is encrypted, so that even if you open it with a text editor and try to look at the PDF code (always a treat), all you see is gibberish.

The encryption applied to the file's contents has become more sophisticated as Acrobat has matured. The more secure your document is, the later the version of Acrobat a reader must have to open it.

To password-restrict access to a document:

1. With the document open, choose File > Properties.

   The Document Properties dialog opens **A**. Click the Security tab.

2. In the Security Method pop-up menu, choose Password Security.

   The Password Security Settings dialog opens **B**.

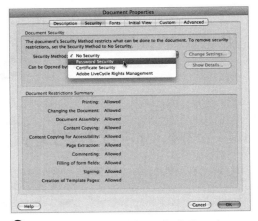

A The Document Properties dialog's Security pane lets you specify what method to use to secure your document.

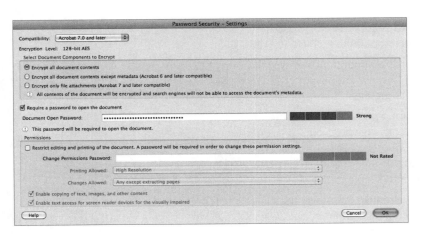

B The Password Security Settings dialog has all the controls to restrict access to your document.

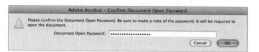

C To prevent your document from being opened by unauthorized personnel, type a password in the Document Open Password text box.

D When you close the Password Security Settings dialog, Acrobat asks you to confirm your password.

3. In the Compatibility pop-up menu, choose the earliest version of Acrobat a reader can have and still be able to open the document.

   Decide how strong the encryption applied to your document must be. Later versions of Acrobat use stronger encryption than earlier versions.

   You can choose compatibility with Acrobat 3, 5, 6, 7, or X. The later the version of Acrobat you require, the harder it will be to illicitly read your encrypted content, but also the more often you'll have readers who can't read your document without updating their Acrobat or Reader software. I find Acrobat 7 compatibility to be a good compromise.

4. Decide what parts within your document should be encrypted: everything, everything except metadata, or nothing except attached files.

   See the sidebar "What to Encrypt?" for a discussion of what to encrypt. Personally, I tend to encrypt everything.

5. Select the "Require a password to open the document" check box.

6. Type a password in the Document Open Password text box **C**.

   The password you type appears as a row of bullets on the screen. A "strength meter" gives you an idea of how secure your password is.

7. Click OK.

   A dialog opens asking you to confirm your password **D**.

continues on next page

8. Type your password into the text box, and click OK.

Acrobat returns you to the Document Properties dialog, which now displays your security settings.

9. Click OK to return to your PDF document.

TIP The document isn't actually password-protected until you save it to your disk. Until then, you can freely change your security settings by clicking the Change Settings button in the Document Properties dialog Ⓐ.

TIP When readers attempt to open your protected file, they're asked for a password Ⓔ. If they type an incorrect password, they aren't allowed to open the file.

Ⓔ Acrobat requests the password from anyone who tries to open your password-protected document.

What to Encrypt?

When you assign an Open password to a document, Acrobat encrypts the contents of the document, making it impossible to read the document without knowing the password. Acrobat gives you three choices when deciding how much of your PDF file to encrypt Ⓕ:

- **Encrypt all document contents.** Acrobat encrypts everything in your file. This is the option I generally choose because it has the lowest requirements for reading the document: A reader can access it with Acrobat 5 or later.

- **Encrypt all document contents except metadata.** Acrobat leaves keywords and other metadata unencrypted so they're searchable. This requires the reader to have Acrobat 6 or later.

- **Encrypt only file attachments.** The Comments pane lets you attach a spreadsheet or other file to your document. These attached files are encrypted, but nothing else is. This requires at least Acrobat 7 to be read.

Select Document Components to Encrypt

⦿ Encrypt all document contents

○ Encrypt all document contents except metadata (Acrobat 6 and later compatible)

○ Encrypt only file attachments (Acrobat 7 and later compatible)

Ⓕ You have control over what parts of your password-protected document are encrypted.

Restricting Activities

Acrobat lets you restrict what users can do with your file once they have opened it. The Permissions controls in the Password Security Settings dialog **A** allow you to restrict the editing and printing of your file, and to assign a password that must be typed in before the permissions can be changed.

These permissions and their password are completely independent of the password needed to open the document. You can have an Open password, a Permissions password, both, or neither.

When protecting your document, you can select among three levels of printing permission:

- **High Resolution.** This option allows unrestricted printing of the document.

- **Low Resolution.** The document is always printed as a 150-dpi bitmap. Thus, a reader can print a proof of this document but not a high-quality copy.

- **None.** The document cannot be printed.

You can also allow one of five degrees of permission for changing the file:

- **None.** The reader isn't allowed to modify the file.

- **Inserting, deleting, and rotating pages.** The reader can change the orientation or presence of pages but cannot modify the contents of those pages.

- **Filling in form fields and signing existing signature fields.** This option is appropriate for a distributed form. It allows recipients to input information in a questionnaire but prevents them from playfully changing the wording of the questions using the editing tools.

- **Commenting, filling in form fields, and signing existing signature fields.** Readers can fill in a form and attach comments. Thus, an expense report form would allow the attachment of scanned receipts (as an "attachment" comment).

- **Any except extracting pages.** Readers can modify the document in any way they wish except pulling the pages out into another document. Note that readers can use the editing tools to change the content of the PDF file.

continues on next page

Permissions

☑ Restrict editing and printing of the document. A password will be required in order to change these permission settings.

Change Permissions Password: ••••••••••••••••• ▢▢▢▢ **Strong**

Printing Allowed: Low Resolution (150 dpi) ⇕

Changes Allowed: None ⇕

☐ Enable copying of text, images, and other content

☑ Enable text access for screen reader devices for the visually impaired

A The Permissions controls let you specify the degree to which readers can edit your document.

In addition to these editing and printing permissions, a check box below the pop-up menus allows readers to copy text and other content from your file, presumably so they can paste it into another document.

Finally, if you restrict copying of the content of your document, you may nonetheless allow screen readers and other devices for the visually impaired to extract the text.

To assign permissions to a document:

1. With the document open, choose File > Properties.

   Acrobat displays the Document Properties dialog 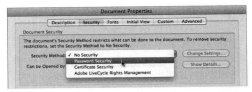.

2. In the Security Method pop-up menu, choose Password Security.

   The Password Security Settings dialog opens.

3. Select the "Restrict editing and printing" check box Ⓐ.

4. Type a password in the Change Permissions Password field.

   As usual, the password you type appears as a row of bullets on the screen and a strength meter provides a measure of its effectiveness.

5. Choose the degree of printing permission you want from the Printing Allowed pop-up menu Ⓒ.

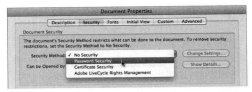

Ⓑ To assign permissions to a document, start by specifying password protection in the Document Properties dialog.

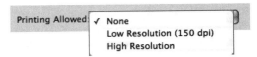

Ⓒ You can forbid a reader to print your document, allow a low-resolution proof, or allow high-quality printing.

Permissions Caveat

One important detail to remember about setting permissions is that obeying the restrictions is the responsibility of the PDF-viewing software, which includes not only the Adobe Acrobat products, but also such programs as Apple's Preview and the free Ghostscript program.

Permissions exist as a series of "flags" in the PDF file that tell the PDF viewer which actions are restricted and which are allowed. Absolutely nothing enforces these restrictions; if a PDF viewer chooses to ignore them, it may allow its user to print, edit, and otherwise modify the PDF file regardless of the permissions settings.

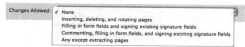

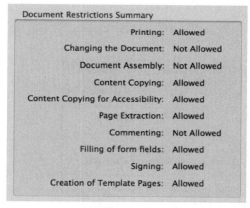

D You can choose from a variety of degrees to which a user can modify your PDF file.

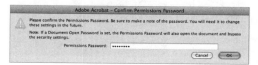

E When you close the Password Security Settings dialog, Acrobat asks you to confirm your password.

Document Restrictions Summary	
Printing:	Allowed
Changing the Document:	Not Allowed
Document Assembly:	Not Allowed
Content Copying:	Allowed
Content Copying for Accessibility:	Allowed
Page Extraction:	Allowed
Commenting:	Not Allowed
Filling of form fields:	Allowed
Signing:	Allowed
Creation of Template Pages:	Allowed

F Once you've saved your document, the Permissions settings are put in place and the Document Properties dialog reflects this.

6. From the Changes Allowed pop-up menu, choose the permission you want to allow for editing your file **D**.

7. If you want to allow readers to copy text and images from your PDF file, select the "Enable copying" check box.

8. If you choose to not allow readers to copy text from your file, but you still want screen readers for the visually impaired to work, select the "Enable text access" check box.

   This check box is disabled if you allow text copying.

9. Click OK.

   Acrobat asks you to confirm your password **E**.

10. Type your password in the text box, and click OK.

    Acrobat returns you to the Document Properties dialog.

11. Click OK to return to the document page.

    The permissions aren't actually set until you save the PDF file. Until then, you can click the Change Settings button in the Document Properties dialog and modify your permissions.

    Once you've saved your file, the Document Properties dialog reflects your security settings **F**.

Redacting a Document

Acrobat Pro Only: *Redaction* refers to marking out or otherwise rendering unreadable sensitive parts of a document, usually to preserve information secrecy. This can be done to protect legal or trade secrets, or to prevent someone's personal information from being broadcast.

In Acrobat X, redaction is a three-step process.

1. You first set the redaction properties, specifying how redacted items appear on the page.

2. Next, you go through the document and choose the text and graphics that should be redacted.

3. You then apply redaction to the marked items. Acrobat replaces each redacted item with a colored block (a *redaction overlay),* optionally containing a text message **A**.

Once redacted, the items are permanently unreadable; the process cannot be undone. (It wouldn't be worth much if it could be undone, now would it?)

This reporter was particularly happy at the timely delivery (in time for the conference) of Exp. Del. No more illustrating conferences with hand drawings! The savings in crayons alone will quickly pay for the new cameras.

A Redacted items in your PDF file are covered with opaque redaction overlays. (Exp. Del. is short for "Expletive Deleted," if you were curious.)

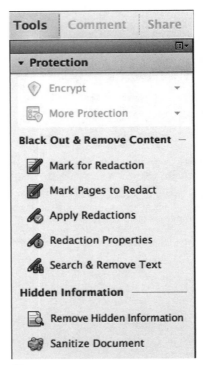

B The redaction tools reside in the Protection panel of the Tools pane.

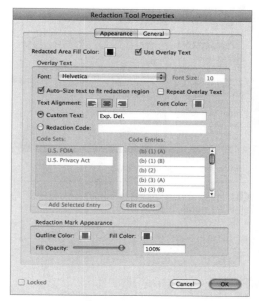

C The Redaction Tool Properties dialog lets you specify the appearance of the redaction overlays.

> **TIP** I always select the "Auto-size text to fit redaction region" check box. Acrobat picks a font size for each redacted item that makes the overlay text exactly fit the overlay.

> **TIP** You'll notice there is another pair of color controls at the bottom of the Redaction Tool Properties dialog **C**. These specify the color of the temporary rectangle the redaction tools put on the page when you are initially marking areas for redaction.

> **TIP** Although you technically don't have to reset the redaction properties for each document you redact, I usually do because I generally want a different label for each document's redaction overlays.

You carry out the redaction process using the redaction tools in the Protection panel of the Tools pane **B**.

Let's first set the redaction properties.

To set redaction properties:

1. In the Protection panel, click Redaction Properties **B**.

   The Redaction Tool Properties dialog opens **C**.

2. Choose the color you want for the redaction overlays by clicking in the color control labeled "Redacted Area Fill Color" and selecting a color from the resulting color picker.

3. If you want to place text into the redaction overlays, select the Use Overlay Text check box.

4. Choose your text characteristics: font, size, color, and alignment.

   Remember that the text color must be readable against the fill color you chose in step 2.

5. If you want to supply your own text for the overlay, type the text in the Custom Text field.

6. If you want to use a standard code to indicate the reason for the redaction, choose one from among the code sets.

   Acrobat provides codes from the U.S. Freedom of Information Act and the U.S. Privacy Act. You can add your own sets of codes, if you want; consult the Acrobat X Help to learn how to do this.

7. Click OK.

To redact items in a document:

1. In the Protection panel, click Mark for Redaction **B**.

   The pointer turns into an I-beam when it's over text and a crosshair when it's over white space in your document.

2. With the I-beam pointer, select all the text that needs to be hidden.

3. With the crosshair, drag enclosing rectangles around artwork or other items that need to be obscured.

   Acrobat draws a rectangle around the marked text and artwork **D**. When the pointer moves over it, the rectangle changes to show the redaction overlay that will be placed there when the redaction is applied **E**.

4. In the Protection panel, click Apply Redactions.

   Acrobat hides all the redacted items with redaction overlays.

   Acrobat then examines your document, looking for other internal information that you may also want to remove for security reasons. Acrobat optionally presents you with the Remove Hidden Information pane **F**, which lists all the comments, bookmarks, electronic signatures, and other data it found in the file.

5. Click the Remove button, if desired.

   Acrobat removes the internal objects from the document and returns you to your now-redacted document page.

   Acrobat marks the newly redacted document as Save-As Only; you must save it with a new name. When you close the document, the standard Save dialog opens, prompting you to save the document.

This reporter was particularly happy at the timely delivery (in time for the conference) of photographic equipment. No more illustrating conferences with hand drawings! The savings in crayons alone will quickly pay for the new cameras.

D Items you've selected for redaction are outlined with a thick border.

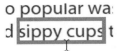 

E When the Select for Redaction pointer moves over a redaction marker, the rectangle changes to show how the final redaction overlay will look.

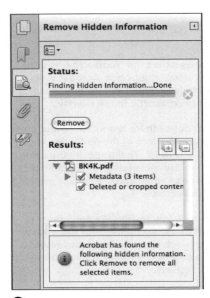

F Having redacted the items you selected, Acrobat searches the document for other, hidden items you may want to remove.

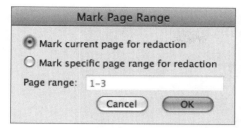

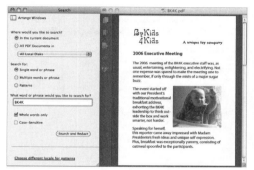

G You can specify an entire page be redacted. You can redact the current page or a specified range of pages.

H Clicking the Search & Redact button lets you specify a word or phrase that should be redacted throughout your document.

TIP While you are marking items for redaction, you can change your mind and remove the mark from an item. To do so, click its marking rectangle, and press the Delete or Backspace key. You need to do this before you apply the redaction.

TIP You can also redact entire pages in the document. Click Mark Pages to Redact in the Protection panel; Acrobat will display a dialog that lets you specify a range of pages to be redacted **G**. Every page of the range you specify will have its entire contents marked for redaction.

Search and redact

As a great convenience, Acrobat searches for words and phrases in your document and redacts all instances of that text. The process is similar to searching for text, as discussed in Chapter 2.

Acrobat can search out and redact three types of text in your document:

- All instances of a particular word or phrase.

- All instances of a list of words or phrases.

- All instances of a particular text pattern (such as social security numbers or telephone numbers).

To redact all instances of a phrase in a document:

1. In the Protection panel, click Search & Remove Text.

   Acrobat opens the Search dialog and zooms your document page out so the two windows (Search and document) together fill your screen **H**. The Search window defaults to searching for a particular phrase.

   continues on next page

2. In the Search dialog's text field, type the phrase or word you want to redact.

3. Click the Search and Redact button.

The Search dialog opens and presents you with a list of instances of the search phrase found in the document ❶. Each item in this list has a check box next to it, indicating that that instance should be redacted.

4. Select the check boxes for all the instances in the list that you want to redact.

You can also click the Check All button to choose all items in the list.

5. Click the "Mark Checked Results for Redaction" button.

Acrobat marks for redaction all selected instances of the text in the document ❿.

6. In the Protection panel, click Apply Redactions.

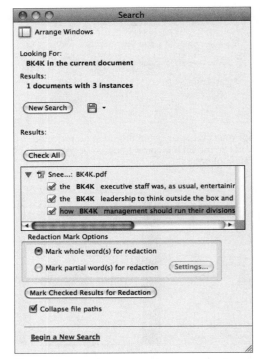

❶ The Search window presents a list of all the instances of the found text. Selecting an item's check box marks the item for redaction.

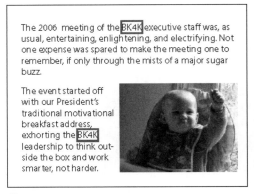

❿ Clicking the Search window's "Mark Checked Results for Redaction" button marks all the selected items for redaction.

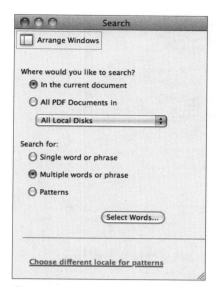

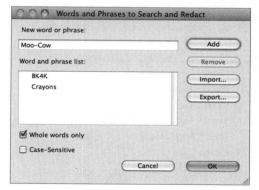

K If you opt to redact multiple words or phrases, Acrobat makes visible a button labeled Select Words.

L The Words and Phrases dialog lets you specify a list of, well, words and phrases that should be redacted in your document.

To redact all instances of a list of words or phrases in a document:

1. In the Protection panel, click Search & Remove Text.

2. In the Search window, click the "Multiple words or phrase" radio button **H**.

   The window rearranges itself, among other things making visible a Select Words button **K**.

3. Click the Select Words button.

   Acrobat presents you with a dialog that lets you create a list of words or phrases that should be redacted **L**.

4. Type a word or phrase into the "New word or phrase" field and then click the Add button. Repeat until you are finished.

   Acrobat adds the words and phrases to the redaction list. The dialog also provides buttons that let you export and import a list of words and remove words from the redaction list.

5. Click OK when you have completed your list.

   Acrobat immediately marks for redaction all instances of any of the words or phrases in your list.

6. In the Protection panel, click Apply Redactions.

To redact all instances of a text pattern in a document:

1. In the Protection panel, click Search & Remove Text.

2. In the Search window, click the Patterns radio button.

   The window rearranges itself, presenting a drop-down menu of standard text patterns 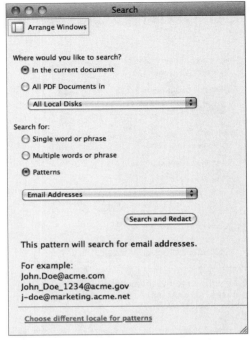.

3. Select a pattern from the drop-down menu **N**.

4. Click the Search and Redact button.

   Acrobat immediately marks for redaction all instances of text matching the pattern you selected.

5. In the Protection panel, click Apply Redactions.

TIP In addition to the redaction features described here, there is a Sanitize Document button at the bottom of the Protection panel **B**. This provides one-click removal of a whole truckload of potentially sensitive items from your PDF file: metadata, obscured text and images, hidden comments, and so on. If a document is worth redacting, it is certainly worth clicking this button.

TIP Keep in mind that if your PDF file contains scanned text, this will not be redacted by the search and redact function. You'll need to redact that text as though it were an image (which it is).

M You can choose to redact all text that fits a particular pattern.

✓ Select your pattern
Phone Numbers
Credit Cards
Social Security Numbers
Email Addresses
Dates

N Acrobat provides a small but useful set of text patterns from which you may choose.

Digital Signatures

From the early days, Adobe has wanted contracts and other agreements in PDF format to be legally binding documents. To do this, there needed to be some way of electronically signing a PDF document so that it was unimpeachably certain that a particular person had agreed to its contents.

This problem has been thoroughly solved. Electronically signed PDF files are accepted as legally binding documents by many federal agencies and state governments, including the Internal Revenue Service and the State of California. In this chapter, you'll learn how to sign a PDF document and how to confirm that the signature on a signed document is valid.

About Adobe Self-Sign Security

Acrobat's electronic signature mechanism is open-ended. Third-party companies, such as Cyber-SIGN and Entrust, can implement their own ways of identifying the signer of a document using Adobe Acrobat's plug-in technology.

In this chapter, we'll discuss the use of the electronic signature mechanism that ships with Acrobat: Adobe Self-Sign Security.

You need to understand the following concepts and terms before you can use Adobe Self-Sign Security:

- **Digital ID.** A collection of data that electronically identifies a person. This data is embedded in a signed document to identify the signer.

- **Certificate.** A file that contains digital ID information. This file can be sent to others for installation into their copy of Acrobat as a trusted identity.

- **Trusted identity.** A certificate that has been installed in your copy of Acrobat and can be used to validate someone else's signature. It's "trusted" in the sense that you know the certificate actually came from the person it's supposed to represent.

- **Signature validation.** The process of confirming that a signature was created with a particular digital ID. When you receive a signed document, validation confirms that the signature was created by one of your trusted identities.

A The tools you use to apply signatures to a document are in the Sign & Certify panel.

Setting up to use signatures

Some preparation must be carried out before you can digitally sign PDF documents. We'll examine each of these steps in detail as we go through the chapter:

- You create on your computer a digital ID that you'll use to sign documents. You must also create a password that you'll use every time you use this ID.

- You create a digital certificate from this ID.

- You send the certificate to people who will be recipients of your signed documents.

- The people to whom you send your certificate must import it into their copies of Acrobat as a trusted identity that represents you as a signer.

   They should also confirm that it was you who sent the certificate, perhaps by calling you on the telephone and asking if you just emailed a certificate to them.

With this preparation in place, signing a document is relatively easy:

- You supply your digital ID and password; the ID's identifying information is embedded in the signature.

- You send your signed document to a recipient.

- The recipient opens the document; Acrobat automatically validates the signature, confirming that it corresponds to your certificate and was, therefore, really placed on the document by you.

You accomplish all this with the tools in the Sign & Certify panel in the Tools pane **A**.

Let's see how to do all this.

Creating a Digital ID

The first bit of preparation you must do when you intend to sign one or more PDF documents is to create a digital ID. You can do this on the fly when you sign a document, but if signing a document will be a common activity for you, you should create your ID ahead of time.

To create a digital ID:

1. In the Sign & Certify panel, choose More Sign & Certify > Security Settings **A**.

   The Security Settings dialog opens **B**.

2. Click the Digital IDs item in the column on the left side of the dialog.

   Acrobat displays all the digital IDs currently defined on this computer. This list is initially empty, of course.

3. Click the Add ID icon.

   The first panel of the Add Digital ID Wizard opens and asks what you want to use to create your ID **C**.

4. Select "A new digital ID I want to create now," and click Next.

   The next panel asks whether you want the ID you create to be stored as a file or in the Windows Certificate Store **D**. For the purpose of this book, the digital file is preferable, because it's a cross-platform industry standard.

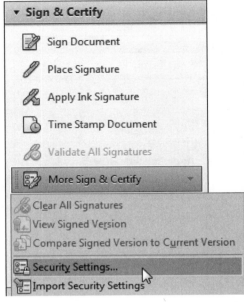

A To create a digital ID, start by choosing Security Settings from the More Sign & Certify submenu.

B You create a digital ID by using the Security Settings dialog.

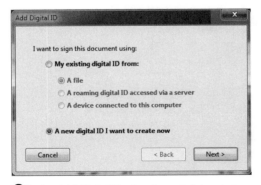

C In the Add Digital ID wizard, you tell Acrobat that you want to make a new self-sign ID.

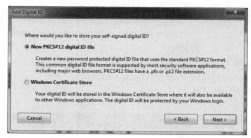

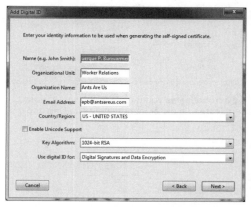

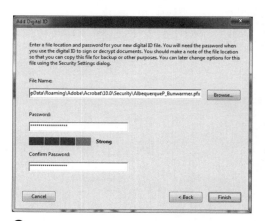

D You can store your digital ID as a standard-format file or in the Windows Certificate Store. The latter works only in Windows, of course.

E You can type in personal information that will be displayed as part of your digital signature. You should supply at least your name.

F Type in a password for the signature; you'll need to supply this whenever you sign a document.

5. Select "New PKCS#12 digital ID file," and click Next.

   The next panel asks for some professional information, such as your name and organization **E**. This information can be displayed as part of your signature.

6. Type in as much of the information as you like (I suggest at least your name), and click Next.

   Acrobat displays the next panel, which asks where the data file for the ID should be placed (there's no good reason not to accept the default). It also asks for a password **F**; this is the password you will supply every time you sign a document.

7. Type a password in the Password and Confirm Password fields, and click Finish.

   When you click the Finish button, Acrobat returns you to the Security Settings dialog, which now displays your new digital ID **G**.

8. Click the window's Close button to finish the process.

G When you return to the Security Settings dialog, it lists your new digital ID.

Creating a Certificate from an ID

A certificate is a file sent to the people to whom you'll be sending signed documents. They import this certificate into their copies of Acrobat to create a trusted identity, which represents you to their systems.

Everyone to whom you send a signed document must have a certificate from you before they can validate your signature.

To create a certificate:

1. In the Sign & Certify panel, choose More Sign & Certify > Security Settings.

   The Security Settings dialog opens **A**.

2. Click the Digital IDs heading in the column on the left side of the dialog.

   Acrobat displays all the digital IDs currently defined on this computer.

3. Select the digital ID for which you want to create a certificate.

   Acrobat displays information about the person whose ID this is.

4. Click the Export icon at the top of the dialog **A**.

   Acrobat displays the Export Options dialog **B**. This presents you with the choice of exporting your certificate as a file or immediately emailing the certificate to someone.

A You create a certificate for your digital ID by clicking the Export button in the Security Settings dialog.

B Acrobat gives you the choice of saving your certificate to a file or immediately emailing it to someone.

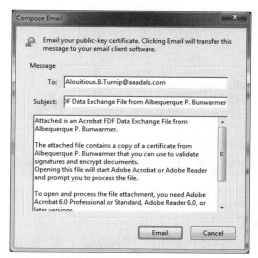

5. Select "Save the data to a file," and click Next.

A standard Save dialog opens.

6. Specify a name and location on your hard disk for the certificate file, and click OK.

Acrobat creates the certificate file in the location you specify. You now have a file that you can send to recipients of your signed documents.

TIP If you select "Email the data to someone" in step 5, Acrobat creates a certificate and immediately emails it to a recipient. When you click the Next button, the Compose Email dialog opens, which lets you supply an address, a subject, and a message body for the email **C**.

C If you have Acrobat email your certificate, the software asks for an address and subject for the email. You can also modify the email's message body.

Importing a Certificate as a Trusted Identity

In the previous section, you created a certificate that encapsulates your digital ID. When you send this file to another person—presumably someone to whom you'll be sending electronically signed documents—that person must import the certificate into Acrobat as a trusted identity.

The presence of a trusted identity allows Acrobat to identify the signer of a PDF document. Acrobat can confirm that a digital signature was placed on the page by the same person who is identified by the trusted identity.

The trusted identity is "trusted" in the sense that you know it really came from the person it claims to represent. This can be confirmed relatively simply: Telephone the person you believe sent you the certificate and ask if that person actually did so.

The following task assumes the certificate file is somewhere on your hard disk, having been emailed to you, perhaps.

To import a certificate as a trusted identity:

1. In the Sign & Certify panel, choose More Sign & Certify > Manage Trusted Identities .

   Acrobat presents you with the Manage Trusted Identities dialog 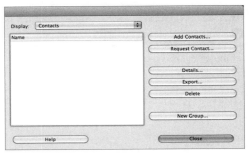. This dialog lists all the trusted identities your copy of Acrobat knows about (none, initially).

A To import a certificate, start by choosing Manage Trusted Identities in the More Sign & Certify submenu.

B In the Manage Trusted Identities dialog, click the Add Contacts button.

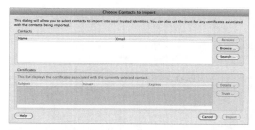

C The Choose Contacts to Import dialog lets you select a certificate to import. Just click the Browse button and select the certificate file.

D Once you've selected a certificate, the name of the contact appears in the Choose Contacts to Import dialog.

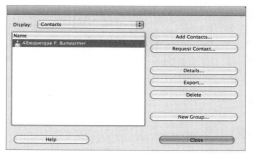

E To specify the actions for which the identity should be trusted, select the contact and click the Details button.

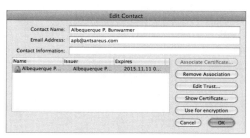

F In the Edit Contact dialog, select the trusted identity and click Edit Trust.

2. Click the Add Contacts button.

The Choose Contacts to Import dialog opens **C**. This dialog allows you to choose one or more certificates to import into your copy of Acrobat.

3. Click the Browse button.

A standard Open dialog opens. Choose the certificate file you want to import, and click OK.

Acrobat returns you to the Choose Contacts to Import dialog, which now lists the certificate you want to import **D**.

4. Click the Import button.

Acrobat returns you to the Manage Trusted Identities dialog, which lists your new trusted signer **E**.

You've now installed a new trusted identity, but you haven't specified what that identity is to be used for; that is, you need to explicitly tell Acrobat that this identity can be used for signatures.

5. Select the newly installed trusted identity, and then click the Details button.

The Edit Contact dialog opens, which presents a list with your installed certificates **F**.

continues on next page

6. Select the certificate you just installed, and click the Edit Trust button.

The Import Contact Settings dialog opens 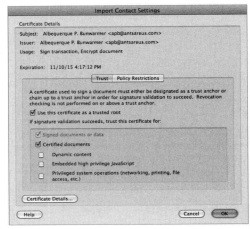. This dialog has check boxes that indicate the purposes for which this identity can be trusted.

7. Select the "Use this certificate as a trusted root" and "Certified documents" check boxes.

You shouldn't select the check boxes for dynamic content, embedded JavaScript, or privileged system operations, because these would allow a signature to "validate" documents that may change dynamically after signing.

8. Click OK to return to the Edit Contact dialog **F** and OK again to return to the Manage Trusted Identities dialog **E**.

9. Click the Close button to close the dialog.

Your copy of Acrobat will now recognize signatures placed on a PDF page by the person whose certificate you imported.

G In the Import Contact Settings dialog, you can specify that the identity should be used to verify signatures.

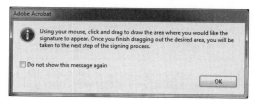

Ⓐ When you first sign a document, Acrobat presents a dialog that reminds you of the procedure.

> 1 of a client and the chances of an "accident" are scurilous lies ely without merit.
>
> **Affix electronic signature here** ➤

Ⓑ The document page usually has a place reserved for your electronic signature.

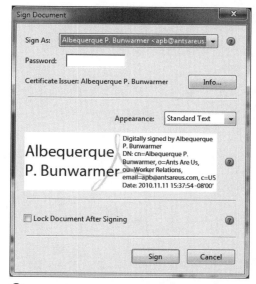

Ⓒ When you sign the document, Acrobat presents you with a dialog that lets you specify the digital ID you want to use and type the corresponding password.

Signing a PDF Document

Having created your digital ID and sent certificates to the appropriate people, the actual signing of a document is pretty easy.

After you've signed a PDF document, Acrobat immediately saves the file in what is called an *increment-only* form. The contents of this type of PDF document cannot be removed from the file. New items can be added to the signed file, but Acrobat can always revert to the original, signed version of the document. This is what makes it possible to use a signed PDF file as a legal document: You can always see the document as it was when people affixed their signatures.

To sign a PDF document:

1. In the Sign & Certify panel, click the Place Signature tool.

   Acrobat reminds you how to place a signature on the page **Ⓐ**.

   This gets annoying after you've signed a few documents, so you should select the "Do not show this message again" check box.

2. Click OK in the reminder dialog to return to your document, where the pointer has changed to a crosshair.

3. Drag a rectangle on the page where you want the signature to go.

   The location of the signature is often a reserved place on a page within the document **Ⓑ**.

   When you release the mouse button, the Sign Document dialog opens **Ⓒ**.

continues on next page

4. Choose a digital ID from the Sign As drop-down menu.

5. Type the ID's password in the Password field.

6. Choose an appearance from the Appearance pop-up menu.

   There is initially only one appearance in this menu: Standard Text. You'll learn how to create new appearances in the next section.

7. Click the Sign button.

   Acrobat presents you with a standard Save As dialog, forcing you to immediately save the signed document.

8. Save the document in the usual fashion.

   Acrobat returns you to the document page, which now has the electronic signature placed on it **D**.

Affix electronic signature here ➧ Albequerque P. Bunwarmer

Digitally signed by Albequerque P. Bunwarmer
DN: cn=Albequerque P. Bunwarmer, o=Ants Are Us, ou=Worker Relations, email=apb@antsareus.com, c=US
Date: 2010.11.11 15:40:32 -08'00'

D When you return to the document page, the signature appears as a bit of text with either your name in large print or a graphic.

E Whenever the signed document is opened, Acrobat will put some text at the top of the window that indicates the document has been signed; there is also a button that opens the Signatures navigation pane.

TIP If the PDF document is a contract or some other document that is intended to be signed, the author will almost certainly place a signature form field on the page, which eliminates a step or two in this process. We'll discuss signature fields later in this chapter.

TIP When you open a signed document, Acrobat places text and a button at the top of the page **E**. The text tells you whether the document's signatures are valid; the button opens the Signatures navigation pane. We'll discuss validating signatures and the Signatures pane later in the chapter.

TIP The Sign & Certify panel also allows you to *certify* a document. This is identical to signing a document, the difference being one of intent. Signing a document means you agree to its contents (as in a contract), whereas certifying means that the document verifiably came from you, not someone else. The mechanics of certifying and signing are the same.

TIP An Apply Ink Signature tool is also in the Sign & Certify panel. When you select this, the mouse pointer becomes a drawing tool that lets you draw on the page, rather like the Pencil tool in many graphics programs. This is useful for computers with a graphics tablet or other pen input device.

Creating a Signature Appearance

By default, the visible representation of a signature on a PDF page is a generic icon accompanied by a collection of text information 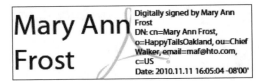. You can change the appearance of the signature, if you'd like: You can specify what information should be presented as text, and you can choose an image or other graphic that becomes part of the signature.

You do this by creating one or more named *appearances* in your Acrobat preferences. An appearance consists of an image and a list of the text information that should visually identify your signature on the page.

When you sign a document, one of the controls that appears in the Sign Document dialog is a pop-up menu of all the appearances available to your copy of Acrobat 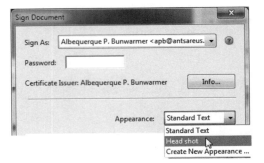. Simply choose the appearance you want to use for the signature.

> **TIP** The marks you see on the PDF page are not the electronic signature: The actual signature is a wad of binary information that is embedded in the PDF file and isn't directly visible on the page. A signature's appearance is just a visible indication that a signature has been placed on the page.

To create an appearance for your signature:

1. In Windows, choose Edit > Preferences; on the Macintosh, choose Acrobat > Preferences.

   The Preferences dialog opens .

2. Select Security in the Categories list on the left side of the dialog.

A Acrobat's default signature comprises a name, the Acrobat icon, and the signer's basic information.

B The Sign Document dialog lets you choose an appearance to use with your signature.

C You create appearances in the Security Preferences.

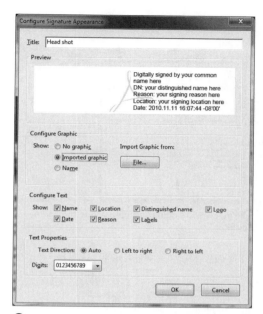

D When you configure an appearance, you specify a graphic to use in your signature and itemize what information should appear in the signature's text block.

E The Configure Signature Appearance dialog presents a preview of what your signature looks like, based on the control settings.

F Your new appearance is in the list in the Security Preferences pane.

3. Click the New button to the right of the Appearance field.

The Configure Signature Appearance dialog opens **D**.

4. Type a name for your appearance in the Title field at the top of the dialog.

This name will appear in the pop-up menu when you sign a document.

5. If you want to have a picture appear as part of your signature, select "Imported graphic," and then click the File button.

An Open dialog opens, letting you select the image, PDF, or other graphic file you want to use for your signature. Acrobat lets you use a wide variety of file types for your signature graphic, including PDF, TIFF, and JPEG files.

6. In the Configure Text section, select the check boxes corresponding to the information you want to appear in the text part of your signature. I recommend at least your name and the date.

The Preview in the dialog reflects your choices **E**.

7. Click OK to return to the Security Preferences, which now lists your new appearance **F**. Click OK again to dismiss the Preferences dialog.

Now, when you sign a PDF document, you can choose your appearance in the Sign Document dialog, and the new signature is displayed on the page using your appearance details **G**.

G When you sign a document, Acrobat applies the appearance you chose to the signature.

Creating a Signature Field

If you're creating a PDF file that contains a contract or other document that must be signed by the reader, you'll make things easier if you provide a signature field as part of the document. This is the electronic equivalent of a "sign here" line on a paper document; when the reader clicks this form field, it presents the Sign Document dialog so the reader can sign the document.

Having created your PDF document, you place a signature field on the page in the Form Editor **A**. (See Chapter 14 for a reminder of the ins and outs of using the Form Editor.)

To create a signature field on a document page:

1. With your document open, in the Forms panel click the Edit button.

   Acrobat displays the document in the Form Editor **A**.

2. Click the Add New Field button and choose Digital Signature **B**.

   The cursor turns into a crosshair.

3. Drag a rectangle on the page, indicating where the signature field should go.

   The field is displayed as an outline with handles and an adjacent palette with a Field Name text field **C**.

4. Type a field name in the Field Name text field.

   The field name can be anything you want, although I suggest you use something appropriate to the field's purpose. The default "Signature1" actually isn't too bad.

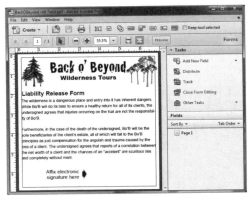

A You create a signature field within the Form Editor.

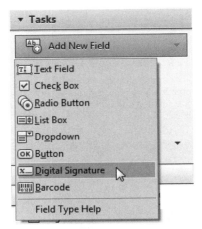

B Choose Digital Signature from the options presented in the Add New Field submenu.

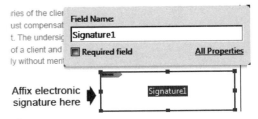

C The signature field initially appears as a rectangle with handles, accompanied by a palette in which you should type a field name.

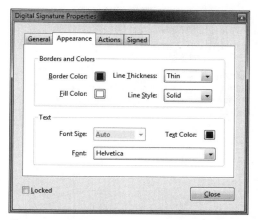

D In the Appearance tab in the Digital Signature Properties dialog, you can specify the color and width of the field's border and fill.

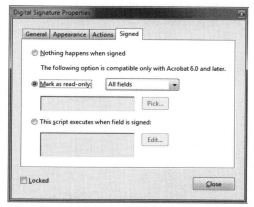

E In the Signed tab, specify what should happen when a signature is fixed to the field.

5. Click the All Properties link. Acrobat displays the Digital Signature Properties dialog **D**.

6. Click the Appearance tab.

7. Use these controls to specify the color you want for the border and fill.

   Black for the border and white for the fill work well. This assumes you don't already have artwork for the field built into the page, in which case you should choose None for these colors.

8. Click the Signed tab.

   Acrobat displays the controls that dictate what should happen when the user signs the document **E**.

9. Select "Mark as read-only," and choose "All fields" in the pop-up menu, which ensures that no further changes can be made after the reader has signed the document.

10. Click the Close button.

    Acrobat returns you to the document page. The new signature field is visible as a rectangle with handles, and the floating palette is now gone.

11. Reposition and resize the field by dragging the rectangle and its handles.

12. Click the Close Form Editing button in the Edit Form mode toolbar to leave Edit Form mode.

continues on next page

The new, functional signature field is visible as a rectangle with a small icon in the upper-left corner ❺. When the pointer moves over the field, it turns into a pointing finger; if you hover over the field for a half second, a tooltip appears, letting the reader know that this is a signature field.

When users click inside the field, the Sign Document dialog opens so they can sign the document.

TIP Instead of locking all fields, as in step 9, you can lock only some of the fields, choosing them from the pop-up menu visible in ❺; you can have nothing in particular happen when the user signs the document; or you can have Acrobat execute a JavaScript when the document is signed. Generally, the most useful action is the one you specified: Lock the document's form fields so no further changes can be made.

TIP As always, it is useful to rummage around among the controls available to you in the Digital Signature Properties dialog ❹. Among other things, you can specify the tooltip that should appear when the user hovers the cursor over the signature field.

TIP You can access a signature (or any other) field's properties anytime you are in the Form Editor by right-clicking (Control-clicking) the field and choosing Properties.

Affix electronic signature here

❺ When you leave the Form Editor, the mouse pointer becomes a pointing finger whenever it passes over the field. Tooltip text appears after a half second.

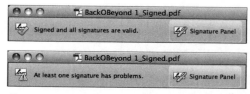

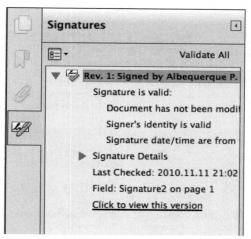

A When you open a signed document, Acrobat supplies one of two messages at the top of the window, indicating that all signatures are valid (top) or that at least one signature may not be valid (bottom).

B The Signatures navigation pane lists all the signatures in the current file, each labeled as valid or not.

Validating a Signed Document

When you receive a signed document, you need to verify that the signature was placed on the page by the correct person. In Acrobat, this means verifying that the signature was placed on the page by someone who is one of your trusted identities. This process is referred to as *validating* the signature.

When you open a signed document, Acrobat automatically compares the digital ID of all the document's signers with your list of trusted identities. If they all match, Acrobat places an appropriate message at the top of the document window **A**.

The validation process happens automatically when you open the signed document. The only time you need to do anything special is if one or more signatures fail to validate, which is indicated by the message "At least one signature has problems," at the top of the document window **A**. In this case, you must validate the signature manually using the Signatures navigation pane, which is located along the left edge of the document window **B**. This pane lists all the signatures in the current document, together with an icon indicating whether each signature is valid.

To validate all signatures in a document:

1. Click the Signatures navigation pane icon to make the pane visible.

2. Click the Validate All link at the top of the pane .

   Acrobat attempts to validate all of the document's signatures, placing a Valid or Invalid icon next to each one in the Signatures pane.

You can still change a signed document using the touch-up and commenting tools. However, even if extensive changes have been made to the document since its signing, it's always possible to revert to the document as it was at signing.

To revert to the original signed version of a document:

1. In the Signatures pane, right-click (Control-click) the signature you're interested in, and choose View Signed Version .

   The document reverts to the signed version; you're looking at the document exactly as it was when it was signed. Acrobat places a notice at the top of the window, telling you that you are looking at an earlier, signed version of the document .

2. Click the View Report button to access a report on any dynamic components (such as JavaScripts) or external dependencies (such as unembedded fonts) in the document that would invalidate the signature.

TIP You should also explore Compare Signed Version to Current Version in the context menu ⓓ. It shows you the signed and current versions of the document side by side, with the differences highlighted. Quite cool.

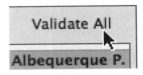

ⓒ To validate all the signatures in the current file, click the Validate All link in the Signatures navigation pane.

ⓓ Using the Options menu in the Signatures navigation pane, you can always see the document exactly as it was when it was signed.

ⓔ Acrobat reminds you that you are viewing the earlier, signed version of a document.

Converting Paper to PDF

Throughout this book we've been discussing the wonderful things you can do with PDF documents; however, most of the important official documents we receive—contracts, estimates, invoices, and the like—are printed on paper. Even Adobe, well into the PDF era, insisted that its developer applications be printed, signed, and faxed back; PDF files weren't accepted. Furthermore, most companies have tons of paper stored in warehouses, documenting many years of transactions and business.

To store these documents on your disk or fill them out electronically, you just scan the paper pages. Because Acrobat can open image files, automatically converting them to PDF, scanned paper documents can be treated entirely as PDF files.

In this chapter, you'll learn how to get the most out of a scanned paper document. Acrobat lets you conveniently fill out scanned paper forms and convert scanned documents into real, searchable text.

Typing on a Paper Form

If you scan a paper form that you need to fill out (or, for that matter, if you receive a PDF-format form that doesn't have form fields), you have a document that looks like a form but, in an Acrobat sense, isn't one. The lines and boxes where you're supposed to write your information are just graphic objects, not interactive form fields that collect information **A**.

You can lay form fields on top of the scanned pages (see "To convert an electronic file into a form" in Chapter 14), but if you need to fill out the form only once and then forget about it, placing form fields on the page is unnecessary work. What you'd like to do is type your responses on top of the page contents, exactly as though you were printing or typing on a paper page.

The Typewriter tool allows you to do exactly that. This is a truly useful little gadget for those of us who prefer to do everything electronically if at all possible. Every time you click the page with the Typewriter tool, a blinking cursor appears, which lets you type text on the page **B**.

This makes it easy to fill in those common, one-off forms that you'll never see or bother with again. The form you fill in can be mailed to another person or, of course, printed and faxed (or emailed; definitely emailed). The typed-on form can be opened with Acrobat 5 or later.

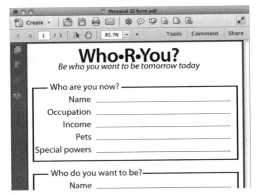

A When you scan a paper form, the result may look like a form, but it isn't, in an Acrobat sense. The lines where you type your data are merely lines, not Acrobat form fields.

Name   Hector B. Nierseited

Occupation   Chicken Counselor|

B The Typewriter tool lets you type text on top of the PDF page, exactly like typing on a paper form.

You open the Typewriter tool by clicking Add or Edit Text Box in the Content panel.

To type form responses onto a PDF page:

1. With the document open, click the Add or Edit Text Box tool in the Content panel **C**.

   The pointer turns into an I-beam cursor and the Typewriter floating toolbar appears **D**.

2. Click the page where you want to type your text.

   Presumably, this will be above or in some graphic element on the page, such as a line or a box.

continues on next page

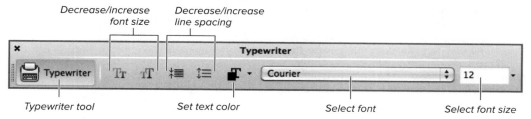

Decrease/increase font size *Decrease/increase line spacing*

Typewriter tool *Set text color* *Select font* *Select font size*

D The Typewriter floating toolbar contains the Typewriter tool and icons that let you select the font, point size, and other text characteristics.

3. Type your text.

If you click the typewritten text with the Typewriter, Select, or Hand tool, Acrobat places a rectangle with handles around the text **E**. You can then reposition the text by dragging the rectangle around the page. You can resize the bounding box of the text by dragging the handles; if you make the box too narrow to accommodate the text, Acrobat wraps it into multiple lines **F**.

TIP You can edit your typewritten text by double-clicking it with either the Hand tool or the Typewriter tool.

TIP The Typewriter toolbar **D** also has icons to change the font, point size, and the spacing between typewritten lines. Click the typewritten text to select it, and then click the icon.

TIP I use the Typewriter tool a *lot.* Anytime I'm sent a paper form from anyone, I scan it, open it in Acrobat, and then fill it out with the Typewriter tool. Not only does this impress the sender with my neatness (it looks way better than my handwriting), but I then have a dated electronic file I can archive.

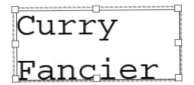

E Having typed your text, you can click it with the Hand, Select, or Typewriter tool to get a border with handles. These let you resize and reposition the text.

**Curry
Fancier**

F If you shorten the text's border too much, the text wraps into multiple lines.

A When you scan a paper page, the result may look like text, but it's really a bitmapped picture of the text.

B In a searchable image, the original bitmap image is unchanged, but there is an invisible layer whose text can be selected, searched for, and copied. Here, we've apparently selected some bitmapped text with the Select tool; in fact, we've selected the underlying real text.

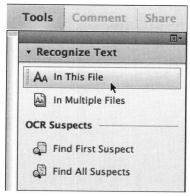

C Acrobat's OCR tools all reside in the Recognize Text panel.

Creating a Searchable Image

When you scan a paper document—a contract, say—the result is a bitmapped picture of the original text and graphics **A**. Although it looks like text, there is, in fact, no text there.

If you're simply reading the document, this technicality doesn't matter; the eye doesn't care if it's looking at text or a picture of text. However, if you're hoping to use common text functions with the document—in particular, if you want to be able to search the document for words or phrases—then a picture of the text won't do. You must have pages of actual text.

Acrobat has a built-in optical character recognition (OCR) function that can analyze an image and convert the picture of the text into real text that can be searched.

The appearance of the page remains the same as the scanned text; the real, searchable text occupies an invisible layer that lies under the scanned text. This preserves the original appearance and relieves Acrobat of having to guess at the font, point size, and other characteristics of the original text. This combination of an image and an invisible text layer is called a *searchable image*.

In a searchable image, all of Acrobat's text-related tools and features (in particular, the Find feature and the Select tool) work as usual and can be applied to the invisible text layer **B**. Thus, in addition to searching for text, you can copy and paste text from the PDF page into another application.

The tools you use to do OCR in Acrobat are all in the Recognize Text panel in the Tools pane **C**.

To create a searchable image PDF file:

1. In the Recognize Text panel, click the In This File tool **C**.

   There's also an In Multiple Files tool, which does what you would expect: presents you with a dialog in which you can select several files for conversion.

   The Recognize Text dialog opens **D**.

2. Choose which pages you want Acrobat to convert.

   You'll nearly always select "All pages."

3. In the Settings section of the dialog, click the Edit button.

   The Recognize Text – General Settings dialog opens **E**.

4. In the PDF Output Style pop-up menu, choose Searchable Image **F**.

5. If necessary, choose the language of the text in the Primary OCR Language pop-up menu.

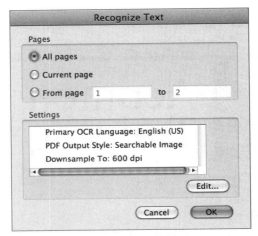

D You specify the pages you want to convert in the Recognize Text dialog. Clicking the Edit button lets you specify the details of the conversion.

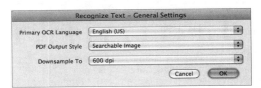

E The Recognize Text – General Settings dialog lets you specify the language and style you want for the OCR process.

F The PDF Output Style menu lets you specify what kind of file should result from the text recognition.

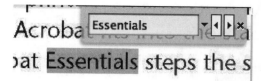

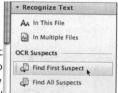

G Having converted your document to a searchable image, you can search for words and phrases within the document.

H The Find Suspect buttons let you step through the instances of scanned text that Acrobat failed to recognize.

6. Click OK to return to the Recognize Text dialog, and click OK once more to have Acrobat convert your document.

   Acrobat analyzes your pages' bitmaps and creates the invisible text layer. When Acrobat is done converting your document, the pages look unchanged. But if you search for a phrase, Acrobat can find it and highlight it **G**.

TIP The PDF Output Style pop-up menu **F** presents two additional choices: Searchable Image (Exact), which is the same as Searchable Image but uses a more sophisticated (and slower) OCR method; and ClearScan, which is an Acrobat feature we'll discuss in the next section. In the context of this discussion, choosing Searchable Image is a good compromise between OCR speed and accuracy.

TIP OCR works best with a 300-dpi monochrome (1-bit, black-and-white) scan. I find it works acceptably with 150-dpi scans, as well. Adobe claims that 72 dpi is adequate, but you'll find some mistakes in the character recognition with such a coarse bitmap.

TIP Sometimes the scanned text is mangled and Acrobat can't make sense of it **H**. The two Find Suspects buttons in the Recognize Text panel let you step through and correct these pieces of problem text. The process is pretty straightforward, so you can explore it on your own.

Converting a Scan with ClearScan

In the previous section, Acrobat created a special, invisible text layer beneath a scanned bitmap. This leaves the scanned image visually unchanged but lets you search for phrases in the scanned text.

Keeping the page as a bitmap maintains the look and feel of the page; however, you cannot edit the text, and zooming in on the text makes it look jagged and unpleasant.

If you'd like to convert your scanned pages into something that can be touched up using Acrobat's editing tools, you need to convert your scan to a combination of actual text and line art, discarding the bitmap altogether. This is the purpose of Adobe's ClearScan feature.

ClearScan was introduced in Acrobat 9, and its accuracy has been greatly improved in Acrobat X. When you convert a bitmap page with ClearScan, the result is a PDF file with real line art and real text. The method of text conversion is very different from what we discussed earlier in the chapter: Acrobat creates a new font on the fly whose metric and artistic characteristics closely match the scanned text. The results are often very good **Ⓐ**.

ClearScan is not appropriate for all circumstances or scanned pages; in particular, if the scan resolution is too low (the exact minimum depending on the font and point size), the new text can look misshapen **Ⓑ**. However, it is still actual text and is scalable, selectable, searchable, and editable.

Ⓐ ClearScan creates a font whose size and other characteristics match those of the font used in the original paper document.

Ⓑ Converting your image with ClearScan can yield misshapen characters; make sure you use a scanned page with a high resolution (300 dpi works very well).

TIP Scan resolution has an enormous effect on the usability of ClearScan results. The paper page in **Ⓑ** was scanned at 100 dpi; compare that with the text in **Ⓐ**, which was converted from a 300-dpi scan. The higher the resolution, the better your converted text will look.

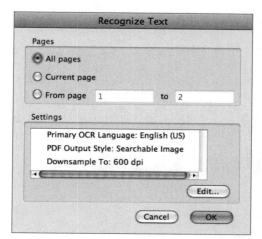

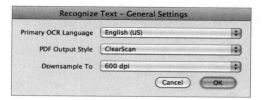

C To use ClearScan, you click the Edit button in the Recognize Text dialog.

D Choose ClearScan in the PDF Output Style pop-up menu.

To convert a scanned document to text and graphics:

1. With the image file open in Acrobat, click In This File in the Recognize Text panel in the Tools pane.

   Acrobat displays the Recognize Text dialog **C**.

2. Select the pages you want Acrobat to convert: all pages, the current page, or a specific range of pages.

   You'll nearly always select "All pages."

3. In the Settings section of the dialog, click the Edit button.

   The Recognize Text – General Settings dialog opens **D**.

4. In the PDF Output Style pop-up menu, choose ClearScan.

5. If necessary, choose the language of the text in the Primary OCR Language pop-up menu.

6. Click OK to return to the Recognize Text dialog, and click OK again to have Acrobat convert your document.

continues on next page

TIP Acrobat can scan a document directly to searchable text. Select the Make Searchable (Run OCR) check box in the Document Settings section of the Acrobat Scan dialog to apply OCR to the scan results **E**. This is extremely convenient if you are converting a large number of paper documents to PDF. See Chapter 4 for a reminder on how to scan paper documents directly to PDF.

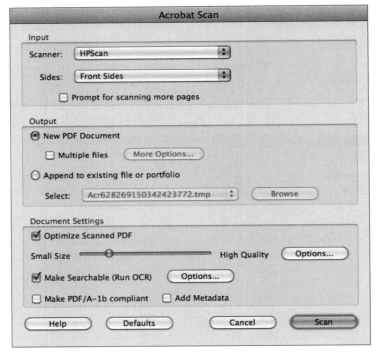

E Click the Make Searchable (Run OCR) check box to scan a paper document directly to searchable text.

Index

WATCH
READ
CREATE

Meet Creative Edge.

A new resource of unlimited books, videos and tutorials for creatives from the world's leading experts.

Creative Edge is your one stop for inspiration, answers to technical questions and ways to stay at the top of your game so you can focus on what you do best—being creative.

All for only $24.99 per month for access—any day any time you need it.

peachpit.com/creativeedge